CCNP Security - SIMOS
Exam (300-209)

Technology Workbook

Implementing Cisco Secure Mobility Solutions (SIMOS)

Associated Certification: CCNP Security

Document Control

Proposal Name	:	CCNP Security SIMOS
Document Version	:	2.0
Document Release Date	:	20-September-2019
Reference	:	CCNP_SEC_WB_SIMOS

Feedback:

If you have any comments regarding the quality of this book, or otherwise alter it to better suit your needs, you can contact us through email at info@ipspecialist.net

Please make sure to include the book's title and ISBN in your message.

About IPSpecialist

IPSPECIALIST LTD. IS COMMITTED TO EXCELLENCE AND DEDICATED TO YOUR SUCCESS.

Our philosophy is to treat our customers like family. We want you to succeed, and we are willing to do everything possible to help you make it happen. We have the proof to back up our claims. We strive to accelerate billions of careers with great courses, accessibility, and affordability. We believe that continuous learning and knowledge evolution are the most important things to keep re-skilling and up-skilling the world.

Planning and creating a specific goal is where IPSpecialist helps. We can create a career track that suits your visions as well as develop the competencies you need to become a professional Network Engineer. We can also assist you with the execution and evaluation of your proficiency level, based on the career track you choose, as they are customized to fit your specific goals.

We help you STAND OUT from the crowd through our detailed IP training content packages.

Course Features:

❖ Self-Paced Learning
  ● Learn at your own pace and in your own time
❖ Covers Complete Exam Blueprint
  ● Prep-up for the exam with confidence
❖ Case Study Based Learning
  ● Relate the content with real-life scenarios
❖ Subscriptions that suits you
  ● Get more and pay less with IPS subscriptions
❖ Career Advisory Services
  ● Let the industry experts plan your career journey
❖ Virtual Labs to test your skills
  ● With IPS vRacks, you can evaluate your exam preparations
❖ Practice Questions
  ● Practice Questions to measure your preparation standards
❖ On Request Digital Certification
  ● On request digital certification from IPSpecialist LTD.

About the Authors:

This book has been compiled with the help of multiple professional engineers. These engineers specialize in different fields e.g. Networking, Security, Cloud, Big Data, IoT etc. Each engineer develops content in his/her own specialized field that is compiled to form a comprehensive certification guide.

About the Technical Reviewers:

Nouman Ahmed Khan

AWS-Architect, CCDE, CCIEX5 (R&S, SP, Security, DC, Wireless), CISSP, CISA, CISM, Nouman Ahmed Khan is a Solution Architect working with a major telecommunication provider in Qatar. He works with enterprises, mega-projects, and service providers to help them select the best-fit technology solutions. He also works as a consultant to understand customer business processes and helps select an appropriate technology strategy to support business goals. He has more than fourteen years of experience working in Pakistan/Middle-East & UK. He holds a Bachelor of Engineering Degree from NED University, Pakistan, and M.Sc. in Computer Networks from the UK.

Abubakar Saeed

Abubakar Saeed has more than twenty-five years of experience, managing, consulting, designing, and implementing large-scale technology projects, extensive experience heading ISP operations, solutions integration, heading Product Development, Pre-sales, and Solution Design. Emphasizing on adhering to Project timelines and delivering as per customer expectations, he always leads the project in the right direction with his innovative ideas and excellent management skills.

Muhammad Yousuf

Muhammad Yousuf is a professional technical content writer. He is a Certified Ethical Hacker (v10) and Cisco Certified Network Associate in Routing and Switching, holding a Bachelor's Degree in Telecommunication Engineering from Sir Syed University of Engineering and Technology. He has both technical knowledge and industry sounding information, which he uses perfectly in his career.

Free Resources:

With each workbook bought from Amazon, IPSpecialist offers free resources to our valuable customers.

Once you buy this book, you will have to contact us at support@ipspecialist.net or tweet @ipspecialistnet to get this limited time offer without any extra charges.

Free Resources Include:

Exam Practice Questions in Quiz Simulation: With more than 300+ Q/A, IPSpecialist's Practice Questions is a concise collection of important topics to keep in mind. The questions are especially prepared following the exam blueprint to give you a clear understanding of what to expect from the certification exam. It goes further on to give answers with thorough explanations. In short, it is a perfect resource that helps you evaluate your preparation for the exam.

Career Report: This report is a step by step guide for a novice who wants to develop his/her career in the field of computer networks. It answers the following queries:

- What are the current scenarios and future prospects?
- Is this industry moving towards saturation or are new opportunities knocking at the door?
- What will the monetary benefits be?
- Why to get certified?
- How to plan and when will I complete the certifications if I start today?
- Is there any career track that I can follow to accomplish specialization level?

Furthermore, this guide provides a comprehensive career path towards being a specialist in the field of networking and also highlights the tracks needed to obtain certification.

IPS Personalized Technical Support for Customers: Good customer service means helping customers efficiently, in a friendly manner. It is essential to be able to handle issues for customers and do your best to ensure they are satisfied. Providing good service is one of the most important things that can set our business apart from the others of its kind.

Great customer service will result in attracting more customers and attain maximum customer retention.

IPS is offering personalized TECH support to its customers to provide better value for money. If you have any queries related to technology and labs, you can simply ask our technical team for assistance via Live Chat or Email.

Our Products

Technology Workbooks

IPSpecialist Technology workbooks are the ideal guides to developing the hands-on skills necessary to pass the exam. Our workbooks cover official exam blueprint and explain the technology with real life case study based labs. The contents covered in each workbook consist of individually focused technology topics presented in an easy-to-follow, goal-oriented, step-by-step approach. Every scenario features detailed breakdowns and thorough verifications to help you completely understand the task and associated technology.

We extensively used mind maps in our workbooks to visually explain the technology. Our workbooks have become a widely used tool to learn and remember the information effectively.

vRacks

Our highly scalable and innovative virtualized lab platforms let you practice the IP Specialist Technology Workbook at your own time and your own place as per your convenience.

Quick Reference Sheets

Our quick reference sheets are a concise bundling of condensed notes of the complete exam blueprint. It is an ideal and handy document to help you remember the most important technology concepts related to the certification exam.

Practice Questions

IP Specialists' Practice Questions are dedicatedly designed from a certification exam perspective. The collection of these questions from our technology workbooks are prepared keeping the exam blueprint in mind covering not only important but necessary topics as well. It is an ideal document to practice and revise for your certification.

Table of Contents

Chapter 1: Secure Communications Architectures.................................13

  Technology Overview...13

    VPN Concept..14

    Types of VPN...15

  Encryption, Hashing and Next Generation Encryption (NGE)...........16

    Cryptography Concepts..16

    Hashing...20

    Public Key Infrastructure (PKI)...23

    Next Generation Cryptographic Encryption..........................28

    Elliptic Curve Cryptography (ECC).......................................31

    SSL DTL and TLS for Secure Communication.........................32

    IPSec..34

  Site-to-Site VPN Solutions...42

    Categories of Site-to-Site VPN Solutions..............................42

    VPN Technology Consideration..43

    Dynamic Multipoint VPN (DMVPN).....................................45

    Flex VPN...51

    Group Encrypted Transport VPN(GETVPN)...........................52

    High Availability Consideration for Site-to-Site VPN Solutions.....58

  Remote Access VPN Solutions..61

    Full Tunnelling VPNs..61

    Clientless VPN...62

    Software Remote Access IPSec VPN (EZVPN)........................64

    Hardware Remote Access IPSec VPN (EZVPN).......................64

    Clientless SSL Browser & Client Consideration......................65

AnyConnect Client Requirements 65

Remote Access VPN Consideration Based on Functional Requirements 68

High Availability Consideration for Remote Access VPN Solutions 70

Split Tunnelling 73

Chapter 2: Secure Communications 75

Cisco AnyConnect Secure Mobility Client Installation 75

Web Deployment Mode 75

Manual Deployment Mode 76

Lab 1.1: Implementing IPv4 IPSec with IKEv1 80

Lab 1.2: Implementing IPv4 IPSec with IKEv2 85

Lab 1.3: Implementing DMVPN IPv4 Hub-Spoke and Spoke-Spoke 92

Lab 1.4: Implementing DMVPN IPv6 over IPv4 96

Lab 1.5: Implementing Site-to-Site Flex VPN 104

Lab 1.6 : Implementing Clientless SSL VPN on ASA 112

Implementing AnyConnet SSL VPN on ASA 120

Implementing Software Remote Access IPSec VPN (EZVPN) 133

Chapter 3: Troubleshooting & Monitoring VPN 141

Troubleshooting VPN 141

Troubleshooting IPSEC IKEv1 based on Configuration Output 141

Troubleshooting IPSEC IKEv2 based on Configuration Output 147

Troubleshooting DMVPN based on Configuration Output 151

Troubleshooting FlexVPN based on Configuration Output 154

References 157

About Our Products 160

About this Workbook

This workbook covers all the information you need to pass the Cisco CCNP 300-209 exam. The workbook is designed to take a practical approach of learning with real life examples and case studies.

- ➢ Covers complete CCNP 300-209 blueprint
- ➢ Summarized content
- ➢ Case Study based approach
- ➢ Ready to practice labs on VM
- ➢ 100% pass guarantee
- ➢ Mind maps

Cisco Certifications

Cisco Systems, Inc. specializes in networking and communications products and services. A leader in global technology, the company is best known for its business routing and switching products that direct data, voice, and video traffic across networks worldwide.

Cisco also offers one of the most comprehensive vendor-specific certification programs in the world, the *Cisco Career Certification Program*. The program has six (6) levels, which begins at the Entry level and then advances to Associate, Professional, and Expert levels. For some certifications, the program closes at the Architect level.

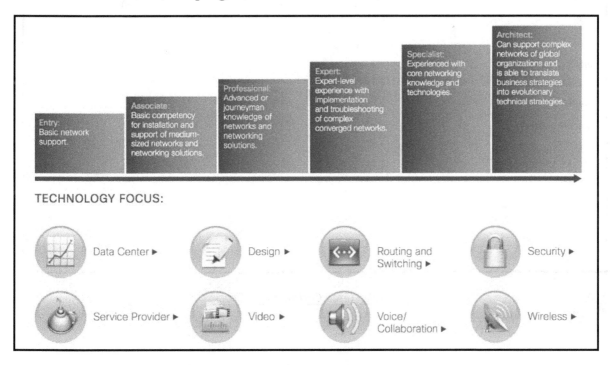

Figure 1- Cisco Certifications Skill Matrix- Copyright 2013 by Cisco and/or its Affiliates

How does Cisco Certifications Help?

Cisco certifications are a de facto standard in networking industry, which helps you boost your career in the following ways:

1. Gets your foot in the door by launching your IT career.
2. Boosts your confidence level.
3. Proves knowledge, which helps improve employment opportunities.

As for companies, Cisco certifications is a way to:

1. Screen job applicants.
2. Validate the technical skills of the candidate.
3. Ensure quality, competency, and relevancy.
4. Improve organization credibility and customer's loyalty.
5. Meet the requirement in maintaining organization partnership level with OEMs.
6. Helps in Job retention and promotion.

Cisco Certification Tracks

Certification Tracks	Entry	Associate	Professional	Expert	Architect
Collaboration				CCIE Collaboration	
Data Center		CCNA Data Center	CCNP Data Center	CCIE Data Center	
Design	CCENT	CCDA	CCDP	CCDE	CCAr
Routing & Switching	CCENT	CCNA Routing and Switching	CCNP	CCIE Routing & Switching	
Security	CCENT	CCNA Security	CCNP Security	CCIE Security	
Service Provider		CCNA Service Provider	CCNP Service Provider	CCIE Service Provider	
Service Provider Operations	CCENT	CCNA Service Provider Operations	CCNP Service Provider Operations	CCIE Service Provider Operations	
Video		CCNA Video			
Voice	CCENT	CCNA Voice	CCNP Voice	CCIE Voice	
Wireless	CCENT	CCNA Wireless	CCNP Wireless	CCIE Wireless	

Figure 2- Cisco Certifications Track

About the CCNP Exam

- **Exam Number:**   300-209 CCNP
- **Associated Certifications:**   CCNP Security
- **Duration:**   90 minutes (65-75 questions)
- **Exam Registration:**   Pearson VUE

The Cisco Certified Network Professional (CCNP) Security Composite Exam (300-209) is a 90-minute, 65–75 question assessment that is associated with the CCNP Security Certification. This exam tests a candidate's knowledge and skill related to technologies used to strengthen and implement the secure communication by using variety of Virtual Private Network (VPN) such as remote access SSL VPN and site-to-site VPN both on Cisco IOS software platform and Firewall appliances.

The following topics are general guidelines for the content likely to be included on the exam:

- Secure Communications: 32%
- Troubleshooting, Monitoring, and Reporting Tools: 38%
- Secure Communications Architectures: 30%

Complete list of topics covered in the CCDA exam can be downloaded here:

http://www.cisco.com/web/learning/exams/docs/300-209_simos.pdf

How to become CCNP Security?

Step 1: Pre-requisites

A valid CCNA Security Certification or any CCIE Certification can act as a prerequisite.

Step 2: Prepare for the CCNA Exam

Exam preparation can be accomplished through self-study with textbooks, practice exams, and on-site classroom programs. This workbook provides all the information and knowledge to help you pass the CCDA Exam. Your study will be divided into two distinct parts:

- Understanding the technologies as per exam blueprint
- Implementing and practicing the technologies on Cisco hardware

IPSpecialist provides full support to the candidates in order for them to pass the exam.

Step 3: Register for the Exam

Certification exams are offered at locations throughout the world. To register for an exam, contact the authorized test delivery partner of Cisco, contact *Pearson VUE*, who will administer the exam in a secure, proctored environment.

Prior to registration, decide which exam to take, note the exam name and number. For complete exam details, refer to the "<u>Current Exam List</u>" from the Cisco website.

Other important details to note are the following:

1. Your personal information prior to exam registration:

    a. Legal name (from government issued ID)

    b. Cisco Certification ID (i.e. CSCO00000001) or Test ID number

    c. Company name

    d. Valid email address

    e. Method of payment

2. If you have already taken a Cisco exam before, please locate your Cisco Certification ID (i.e. CSCO00000001) before continuing with your registration to avoid duplicate records and delays in receiving proper credit for your exams.

3. A valid E-mail is required during exam registration. Cisco requires this in order to send E-mail reminders when a candidate's certification is about to expire, confirm the mailing address before shipping out the certificate, and to inform candidates if their certificate was returned due to an incorrect address.

4. Pearson VUE is the authorized test delivery partner of Cisco. You may register online, by telephone, or by walk in (where available).

How Much does an Exam Cost?

Computer-based certification exam (written exam) prices depend on scope and exam length. Please refer to the "<u>Exam Pricing</u>" webpage for details.

Step 4: Getting the Results

After completing an exam at an authorized testing centre, you will get immediate online notification of your pass or fail status; a printed examination score report that indicates your status, as well as your exam results by section.

Congratulations! You are now CCNP Security Certified.

Chapter 1: Secure Communications Architectures

Technology Overview

One of the important aspects of network security is providing Confidentiality, Integrity, and Availability of data in motion such as an end-user accessing an organization's resources from home or café over the public internet. If this data session is clear text in nature, anyone with little technical skill can sniff critical data worth millions of dollars. An attacker can also modify the data if financial gain is not what they want. By the term *public internet*, it means any kind of network, which is not controlled by the organization. For example, some other autonomous system or group of devices being administered by some other organization or even network administrator, private network like MPLS provider or even some leased line network like Frame Relay.

Similarly, when a small business organization has multiple offices and they cannot afford leased lines connecting to remote offices, they cannot risk sending their critical data off to public internet without any kind of encryption. *Virtual Private Network (VPN)* comes in to play in such situations where a networking staff wants to implement confidentiality, integrity of mobile data off to public internet, or some other autonomous system with minimum expenses.

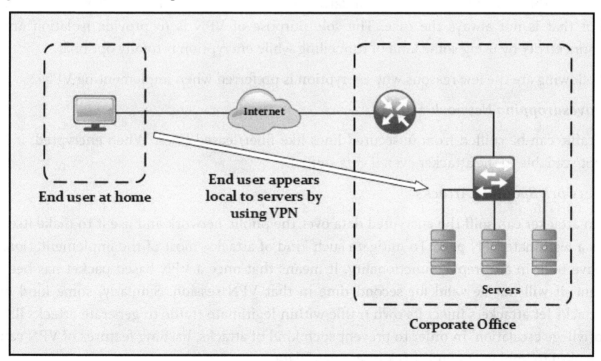

Figure 3- Example of Using VPN for Secure Connection

VPN Concept

Why do we Need VPNs?

Using VPN in enterprise or home environment provides many benefits. Few of them are:

Security

VPN uses one of the most advanced encryption and hashing algorithms to provide Confidentiality and Integrity. Although the latest web browsers have native support for SSL, Cisco's AnyConnect SSL client software also provides SSL based VPN solution. The second most common option is IPSec. It is used for Site-to-Site VPN implementation.

Cost

Connecting remote offices to the most feasible internet service provider and then using VPN for secure connection is so far the most cost effective solution as compared to point-to-point leased lines.

Scalability

Setting up VPN connectivity of newly-established remote office with corporate office is quick in terms of setup than using leased lines.

Why do we Need to Secure VPNs?

Most of the time, it is considered mandatory to use encryptions while implementing VPN, but that is not always the case. The sole purpose of VPN is to provide isolation and connectivity by using some kind of tunnelling while encryption is totally optional.

Following are the few reasons why encryption is preferred when implementing VPNs:

Eavesdropping Network Attacks

Traffic can be sniffed from unsecured lines like fiber/leased lines. When encrypted, it is not readable to the attacker even if gets sniffed.

Network Spoofing Attacks

An attacker can sniff the encrypted data over the public network and use it to make itself as a legitimate VPN peer. To mitigate such kind of attacks, most of the implementations have built in anti-replay functionality. It means that once a VPN based packet has been sent, it will not be valid for second time in that VPN session. Similarly, some kind of attacks let attackers inject its own traffic within legitimate traffic to generate attacks like privilege escalation. In order to prevent such kind of attacks, hashing features of VPN can be used to implement and check integrity of data.

Man-in-The-Middle-Attacks

Sometimes, an attacker gets in-line with normal flow of traffic just to sniff the critical information. In order to prevent such attacks, hashing and encryption along with source authentication needs to be enabled.

Types of VPN

There are two broad types of VPNs being expected in 300-209 certification exam:

Site-to-Site VPN

Allows secure connection of corporate office with branch offices, remote offices or even between multiple businesses. Static or dynamic IPv4/IPv6 address may be assigned to VPN gateways (discussed later) being used in VPN connection.

Remote VPN

Let end user connect to corporate network and use almost any business application by emulating as corporate office computer. Depending on deployment technique, remote VPN may require installation of client software on end-machine. Static IPv4/IPv6 address is assigned to VPN gateway while end-user normally has dynamic IP addressing. If static IP address is not assigned to VPN gateway, then end-user needs Fully Qualified Domain Name (FQDN) of VPN gateway in order to connect to it, but it is not commonly implemented.

The following diagram illustrates these types of VPN:

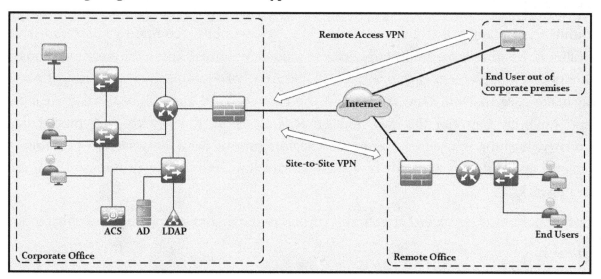

Figure 4- Types of VPN

Mind Map

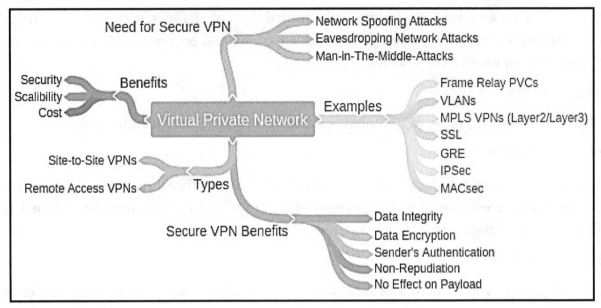

Figure 5- Types of VPN's Mind Map

It is a good idea to review the basic concepts related to cryptographic before moving to next section, as they are important to understand the VPN technologies and their underlying process.

Encryption, Hashing and Next Generation Encryption (NGE)

Cryptography Concepts

Confidentiality, Integrity, and Availability are the three basic components around which we should build and maintain our security model. We must know different methods by which we can implement each one of these features. For example, by using encryption, we can make sure that only the sender and the receiver have the ability to read clear text data. Anybody between the two nodes needs to know the key to decrypt the data. Similarly, hashing is used to make sure the integrity of data. This section explains the concepts and different methods by which we can implement encryption and hashing in our network.

But first, let us define several terminologies before moving to main subject of this section:

Cyphers

A cypher is a set of rules by which we implement encryption. Thousands of cypher algorithms are available on the Internet. Some of them are proprietary, while others are open source. The common methods by which cyphers replace original data with encrypted data are:

- *Substitution*

In this method, every single character of data is substituted with another character. A very simple example in this regard would be to replace the character by shifting three characters ahead of it. Therefore, "D" would replace "A" and so on. To make it more complex, we can select certain letters to be replaced in the whole text. In this example, the value of key is three and both nodes should know it, otherwise, they would not be able to decrypt the data

Similarly, there may be *one to one mapping* of each alphabet (including special characters) for substitution.

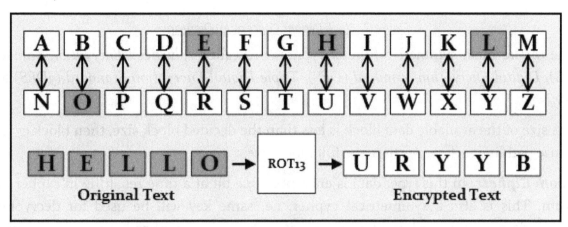

Figure 6- ROT13 an Example of Substitution Cypher

The figure above shows ROT13, a substitution cypher in which every character gets replaced by next 13th character.

1. *Polyalphabetic*

This method makes substitution even more difficult to break by using multiple character substitution.

2. *Keys*

In the above example of substitution, we used a key of "next 13th character". Key plays the main role in every cypher algorithm. Without knowing the key, data cannot be decrypted.

Types of Cyphers

There are two basic types of cyphers:

➤ **Block Cyphers:** In block cyphers, a block or specific chunk of data is encrypted at a time. For example, block size of 1024 bits will encrypt 1024 bits of data into cypher text at a time. In this type of encryption, same key is used for decryption. This type is also known as symmetrical block cyphers.

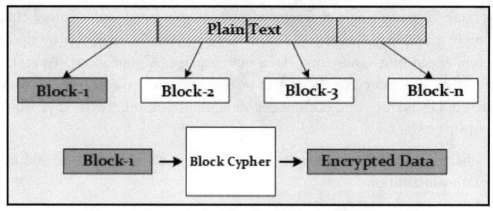

Figure 7- Block Cypher Conceptual Diagram

Some of the main symmetrical block cyphers are called *Advanced Encryption Standard (AES), Digital Encryption Standard (DES), Triple Digital Encryption Standard (3DES)* and *Blowfish.*

If the size of the available data block is less than the decided block size, then block cypher will use padding techniques to make full block size.

> **Stream Ciphers:** In this type, data is encrypted one bit at a time resulting in cypher text stream. This is also a symmetrical cypher; i.e. same key will be used for decryption. Because data is encrypted one bit at time, it makes fewer overheads than block cyphers because no padding technique is used in this case.

Symmetrical encryption algorithms are used in most of the VPNs we use today for data encryption. One of the reasons symmetrical algorithms are preferred is their ability to encrypt data in bulk, which is less CPU intensive as compared to bit by bit encryption. A longer key is generally preferred because the longer the key the more difficult it is to intercept it by using methods like brute-force.

Asymmetric Algorithms

In asymmetric algorithms, a pair of public and private key is used for encryption and decryption respectively. The owner device of public/private key pair only knows the *private key*. A public key will be published online to be used by everyone to make secure connections with that device. As encryption and decryption is a CPU intensive process, so these types of algorithms are used only for things like VPN peer authentication, which may be required at the start of making a connection.

Here are some of the examples of asymmetric algorithms:

Rivest, Shamir, Adleman (RSA)

This algorithm is named after its creators, namely Rivest, Shamir, and Adleman, also known as Public Key Cryptography Standard (PKCS) #1, the main purpose for its usage

today is authentication. The key length varies from 512 to 2048 with 1024 being the preferred one.

Diffie-Hellman (DH)

Diffie-Hellman key exchange protocol is asymmetrical algorithm that allows two peers to share keys over untrusted network. DH is asymmetrical in nature but the keys it generates are symmetric in nature, which in return, are used by symmetrical cyphers like AES, DES etc.

Asymmetric vs. Symmetric Algorithms

Asymmetric algorithms use more CPU processing power than symmetric ones, which makes them more secure. The typical key length used in asymmetric algorithm is between 2049 to 4096. A commonly used asymmetric algorithm for authentication is RSA.

Attributes	Symmetric	Asymmetric
Keys	One key being shared between two or more peers. Key size depends on specific algorithm	Each peer has its own public/private key pair. Key size depends on specific algorithm
Keys Exchange	Out-of-band	Key is exchanged in encrypted form within special message
Speed	Less complex algorithm, hence faster in performance	Complex algorithm results in more CPU usage and slow speed
Number of Keys	Grows exponentially with number of users	Grows linearly with number of users
Security Services Provided	Confidentiality	Confidentiality, non-repudiation and authentication
Examples	DES (64-bit Key) 3DES (168-bit Key) AES (128/192/256-bit Key)	RSA DH Elliptic Curve Cryptography (ECC)

Table 1- Symmetric vs Asymmetric Algorithms Comparison

Hashing

Hashes are used to check the integrity of data. A hash function takes a small block of data and creates a fixed value known as *hash value* or *message digest*. If two computers take same block of data and use same hash function on it, they should get the same hash value. A typical example of hash value is whenever we download some piece of software from internet, an md5 hash is given along with download link to verify the authenticity of software.

The three most popular hash functions are:

Message Digest 5 (MD5)

Hashing is the technique to ensure the integrity. Hash value is calculated by computing specific algorithms to verify the integrity that the data was not modified. Hash values play an important role in proving the integrity not only of documents and images but also used in protocols to ensure the integrity of transporting payload. The Message Digest (MD5) is a cryptographic hashing algorithm, which produces a 128-bit hexadecimal output value. For example, to understand the MD5 of a syntax observe the figure below.

The syntax is:

The password is 12345

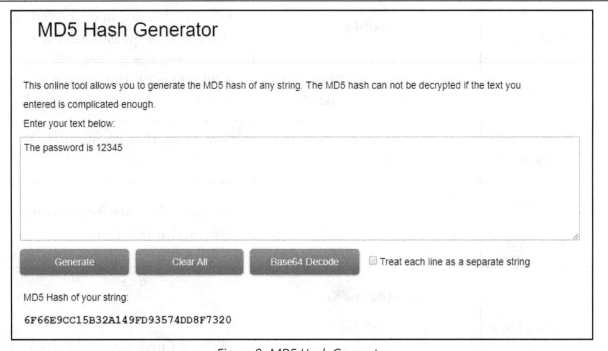

Figure 8- MD5 Hash Generator

Now, observe the output by modifying the content.

The modified syntax is:

> **The password is 1234**

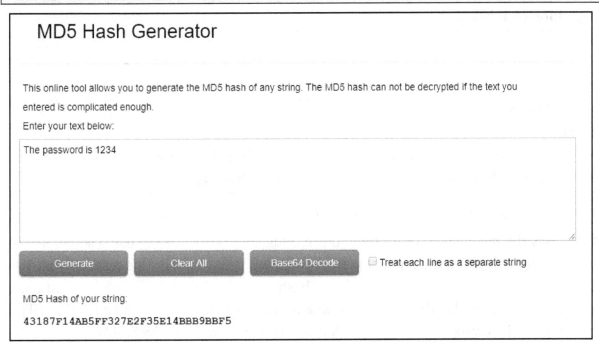

Figure 9- MD5 Hash Generator

As shown, difference of a single alphabet creates a big change in its Hash value, hence any modification in the payload can be detected by comparing the received hash value and the calculated hash value.

Secure Hash Algorithm 1 (SHA-1)

As Message Digest 5 (MD5) is a cryptographic hashing algorithm, another most popular, more secure and widely used hashing algorithm is Secure Hashing Algorithm (SHA). SHA-1 is a secure hashing algorithm producing 160-bit hashing value as compared to MD5 producing 128-bit value. However, SHA-2 is an even more secure, robust and safer hashing algorithm.

> Syntax: **The password is 12345**
> SHA-1: **567c552b6b559eb6373ce55a43326ba3db92dcbf**

Secure Hash Algorithm 2 (SHA-2)

SHA2 has an option to vary digest between 224 bits to 512 bits. SHA-2 is a group of different hashes including SHA-256, SHA-384 and SHA 512. If the cryptographic algorithm is stronger, it will minimize the chances of compromise.

> Syntax: **The password is 12345**
> SHA-256: **5da923a6598f034d91f375f73143b2b2f58be8a1c9417886d5966968b7f79674**

Syntax: **The password is 12345**

SHA-384:

929f4c12885cb73d05b90dc825f70c2de64ea721e15587deb34309991f6d57114500465243ba08a554f8fe7c8dbbca04

Syntax: **The password is 12345**

SHA-512:

1d967a52ceb738316e85d94439dbb112dbcb8b7277885b76c849a80905ab370dc11d2b84dcc88d61393117de483a950ee253fba0d26b5b168744b94af2958145

Hashed Message Authentication Code (HMAC)

HMAC uses the mechanism of hashing, but it adds another feature of using secret key in its operation. Only the two peers know this secret key. Therefore, in this case, only parties with secret keys can calculate and verify the hash. By using HMAC, if there is an attacker who is eavesdropping, he/she will not be able to inject or modify the data and recalculate the correct hash because he/she will not know the correct key used by HMAC.

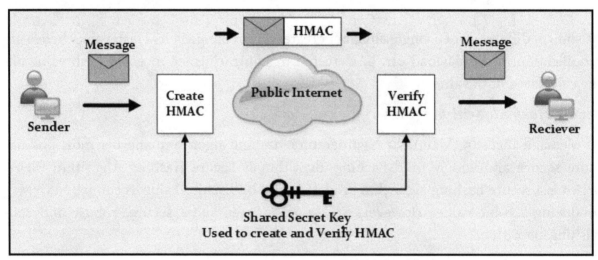

Figure 10- HMAC Working Conceptual Diagram

Digital Signatures

In real setting, signatures are used to prove someone's identity or its commitment towards some task. In computer networks, digital signatures provide three main benefits: *Authentication, Data Integrity* and *Non-repudiation.*

Digital certificates use the methods of hashing and encryption as defined earlier. For example, if Bob and Chris want to make a VPN connection, then they will use digital certificates to make sure that they are talking to a right device.

Let us say that Bob wants to prove his identity to Chris. In the first step, both Bob and Chris will generate their own public/private key pairs, and both have been given digital certificate via common certificate authority. A *certificate authority* is an entity in charge of handing out digital certificates. Inside a digital certificate, there is a public key and a name of device to which it may belong. To create a digital signature, Bob takes a packet and creates a hash. Then Bob takes this hash and encrypts it by using its own private key. When this encrypted hash is sent to Chris, it becomes a *digital signature*.

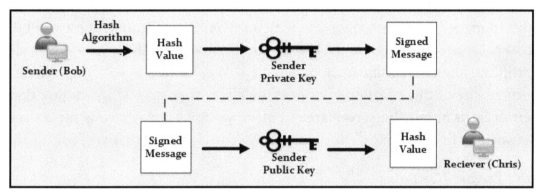

Figure 11- Digital Signature's Working Conceptual Diagram

When Chris receives this packet, he uses Bob's public key (received via Bobs digital certificate) to decrypt this hash. In second step, Chris runs the same algorithm on the remaining packet to calculate another hash. If both of these hashes are the same, it means integrity of data is rock solid.

Public Key Infrastructure (PKI)

PKI is the combination of policies, procedures, hardware, software, and people that are required to create, manage and revoke digital certificates.

Before moving to original discussion, basic terminologies need to be explained:

IPsec

IPsec is used to protect IP packets and it is used both for remote access VPNs and Site-to-Site VPNs. Another option is to use SSL with remote access VPN. In general, IP security (IPsec) is the combination of algorithms to protect IP packets at Layer 3 of TCP/IP model. For encryption, we can use AES, DES, and 3DES. For hashing, we can use MD5 and SHA. For authentication algorithms, which is used to check peers' identity, we can use pre-shared keys and RSA digital certificates.

Below are two primary methods of implementing IPsec:

- **ESP and AH**: Encapsulating Security Payload (ESP) and Authentication Header (AH) are used to implement features of IPsec. The only difference between the two

is that AH does not support encryption. That is why in most of the cases, we use ESP

- **SSL**: In corporate environment, we can implement the security of corporate traffic over the public cloud by using site-to-site or remote VPN. In public network, there is no IPsec software running. Normal users also need to do encryption in different cases like online banking, electronic shopping etc. In such situations, SSL comes into play. The good thing about Secure Socket Layer (SSL) is that almost every single web browser in today's use supports SSL. By using SSL, web browsers will make an HTTPS based session with server instead of HTTP. Whenever a browser tries to make HTTPS based session with a server, a certificate request will be sent to the server in background. The server in return, will reply with its digital certificate containing its own public key. Web browser will then check the authenticity of this certificate with Certificate Authority (CA). Assuming that the certificate is valid, the server and web browser will now have a secure session between them

Public and Private Key Pair

The Public and Private Key pair works like a team in encryption/decryption process. Public key is exchanged with everyone, while private key is kept secret. Every device makes sure that no one has its private key. We encrypt data sending to a particular node by using its public key. Similarly, private key will be used to decrypt the data. This is also true in opposite case. If a node encrypts a data with its private key, then public key will be used for its decryption.

Certificate Authorities

A Certificate Authority (CA) is a computer or entity that creates and issues digital certificates. Number of things like the IP address, fully qualified domain name, and public key of particular device will be present in digital certificate. CA also assigns serial number to digital certificate and signs the certificate with its own digital signature.

Root Certificate

Root certificates are provided by the public key and other details of CA. Following figure shows the example of one:

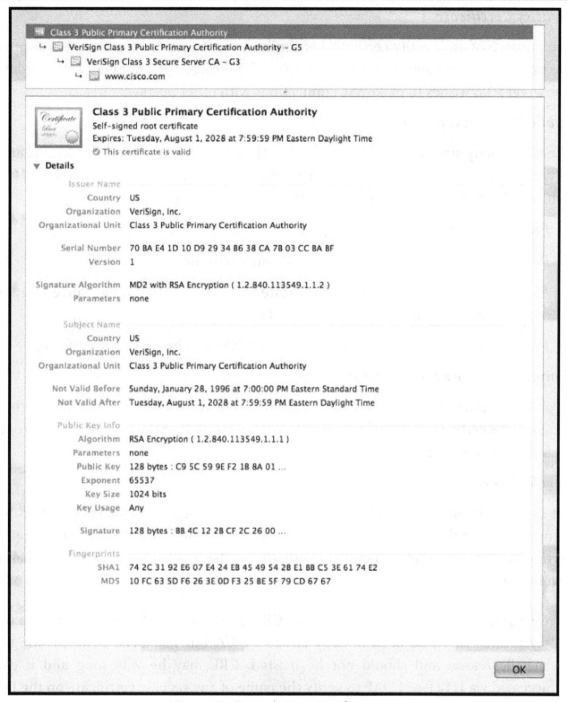

Figure 12- Example Root Certificate

There are multiple informative sections as shown above, which include the serial number, issuer, country and organization names, validity dates, and public keys itself. Every OS has its own placement procedure regarding the certificates. Certificate containers for a specific OS can be searched from the Internet in order to get the certificates stored in the local computer.

Identity Certificate

The purpose of an identity certificate is similar to root certificate except that it provides the public key and identity of client computer or device. For example, a client router or webserver who wishes to make SSL connections with other peers.

Public Key Cryptography Standards

There are many standards available for PKI. These standards control the format and use of certificates. These standards also have Public Key Cryptographic Standards (PKCS) numbers. Some of the important PKCS standards in use today are:

- *PKCS#1*- Standard for RSA cryptography

- *PKCS#3*- Standard related to Diffie-Hellman key exchange

- *PKCS#10*- States the format of certificate request sent to CA for corresponding in order to apply for digital identity certificate

- *PKCS#7*- This format states CA response to PKCS#10 with identity certificate

Simple Certificate Enrolment Protocol

In order to automate the creation and installation of certificates, Cisco, along with other vendors, created Simple Certificate Enrolment protocol. It makes installation of root and identity certificate very convenient.

Revoked Certificates

Let us say an identity certificate has been issued to a device and either this certificate gets compromised or this device is no longer in use, CA can be contacted to revoke the issued certificate. The three most popular methods to check whether a certificate has been revoked or not are:

- *Certificate Revocation List (CRL)*. CRL lists the serial number and names of certificates that had been initially issued by CA but had been revoked due to any specific reason and should not be trusted. CRL may be very long and it can be accessed via HTTP or LDAP to verify the name of any specific certificate on the list

- *Online Certificate Status Protocol (OCSP)*. Client can send requests to OCSP for specific certificate and get response without checking the whole list in case of CRL

- *Authentication, Authorization, and Accounting (AAA)*. AAA service in Cisco also provides the means to validate a certificate but it is not used in PKI due to its proprietary nature

PKI Topologies

There is no universal solution to implement PKI. It depends on network scenario. As number of devices increases, we may have to go from single CA to multiple CAs option as defined below:

Single Root CA

Having a single root CA may work well in small organizations, but as number of devices increases, like 40,000 or more, load on single server increases, which may affect the communications going on over the network. Although CA is not involved directly in every communication, it is a good idea to shift things like CRLs to other servers. Overall, it is a good practice to have some fault tolerance in PKI i.e. to have more than one root CA server.

Hierarchical CA with Subordinate CAs

In order to have fault tolerance in our PKI we need multiple-root CAs. To have some chain of authority, we have one root at the top of the command and multiple subordinate CAs. Root CA gives permission to subordinate CAs, which in turn has abilities to issue identity certificates to clients. In this scenario, clients need to have both root certificate and subordinate CA's certificate. Root certificate is used to verify the digital signature of subordinate CA. In case of multiple subordinate CAs, clients need to have certificates of all subordinate CAs all the way up to root certificate.

Putting it All Together

In summary of the concepts discussed, consider an example of a secure E-mail between Chris and Laurel.

- In order to implement encryption on E-mail, a pair of keys will be used namely Public/Private Key pair

- Chris will encrypt the message with Laurel's public key and send it to Laurel

- Let us say a third person, Mr. Snape was sniffing the data but he would not be able to decrypt and read the message unless he has Laurel's private key

- On reception, Laurel will use her private key to read the original message. Private key must not be shared with anyone except the owner

- Now, this public key is shared inside something called digital signature. A digital signature makes sure that only a legitimate user can read the original data and end-user can verify that no one has changed the data on its way

- In order to understand how a user can make sure of the integrity of data, let us take a simple example of sending a list of numbers to someone over the phone call. Assume that 100 different numbers were written down. In order to verify that all numbers were successfully heard and written down by the person on the other side of phone call, a total number will be reminded to make sure that he/she knows the total amount of numbers he/she is assumed to have received

- In digital world, users make sure the integrity of data by using hashes for digital signatures. As an example, let us assume this sentence as the data that Chris is sending to Laurel over the public internet

"The quick brown fox jumped over the lazy hound"

One of the basic hash techniques would be to add all characters and at the end of sentence, this number should be included as shown below:

"The quick brown fox jumped over the lazy hound. 46"

The sentence above shows that anything between $ signs at the end of message will be the hash of data that is received. Now, the end-user after receiving it, can sum the total characters and if it adds up to 46, then it means that length of data that was received is correct. In reality, very complex algorithms explained in the previous topic, are used to perform the hashing of data. The given example only tells about the length of data. Someone may change the message on its way to receiver and change the hashing part. To prevent such situations, hashed code is sent by some secure channel.

Let us say that private key is used to encrypt the hash code, only public key will be used to decrypt the hash, which is available to everyone on public internet. If attacker wants to modify the hash, then private key would be needed which is only known to the owner of original message. In this way a hashing key along with message is secured by using digital signatures and certificates.

Next Generation Cryptographic Encryption

Over the years, multiple cryptographic algorithms have been created and used in numerous protocols and functions. Most of the algorithms were designed in accordance to the current technology and computational power of computers at that time. Although these algorithms are still supported in latest hardware due to interoperability issues, with the advancements in the field of computer sciences where parallel processing and quantum computing has changed, and with the computational possibilities of computing devices, these algorithms and key sizes are not adequate to mitigate modern attacks and threats.

This table summarizes the recommendation from Cisco Systems Inc. regarding the choice of protocol for hashing and encryption. It should be kept in mind that these protocols are

not used for data encryption/protection. It is for protecting key negotiation process before the start of VPN process.

Algorithm	Operation	Status	Alternative	QCR
DES	Encryption	Avoid	AES	-
3DES	Encryption	Legacy	AES	-
RC4	Encryption	Avoid	AES	-
AES-CBC mode	Encryption	Acceptable	AES-GCM	256-bit
AES-GCM mode	Authenticated Encryption	NGE	—	256-bit
DH-768, -1024	Key Exchange	Avoid	DH-3072	—
RSA-768, -1024	Encryption		RSA-3072	—
DSA-768, -1024	Authentication		DSA-3072	—
DH-2048	Key Exchange	Acceptable	ECDH-256	—
RSA-2048	Encryption		—	—
DSA-2048	Authentication		ECDSA-256	—
DH-3072	Key Exchange	Acceptable	ECDH-256	—
RSA-3072	Encryption		—	—
DSA-3072	Authentication		ECDSA-256	—
MD5	Integrity	Avoid	SHA-256	—
SHA-1	Integrity	Legacy	SHA-256	—
SHA-256	Integrity	NGE	SHA-384	—
SHA-384			—	
SHA-512			—	
HMAC-MD5	Integrity	Legacy	HMAC-	—

			SHA-256	
HMAC-SHA-1	Integrity	Acceptable	HMAC-SHA-256	—
HMAC-SHA-256	Integrity	NGE	—	
EDCH-256 ECDSA-256	Key Exchange Authentication	Acceptable	ECDH-384 ECDSA-384	— —
ECDH-384 ECDSA-384	Key Exchange Authentication	NGE	— —	— —

Table 2- Recommendation Regarding Choice of Protocol

Avoid

Algorithms marked as *avoid* are vulnerable to modern attacks and should not be used to protect sensitive information. These algorithms should be replaced with newer and stronger algorithms wherever possible.

Legacy

Algorithms marked as *legacy* provide acceptable security level. Such algorithms should only be used in situations where interoperability is required or in case of device's limitation etc.

Acceptable

These algorithms are safe from modern attacks and provide adequate security level.

Next Generation Encryption

New algorithms have been designed in order to meet the security and scalability requirements for the next two decades.

Quantum Computer Resistant (QCR)

Parallel processing and quantum computing has been considered as serious threat to previously used hashing and encryption algorithms. Although no one has publically demonstrated any kind of exploits by using such computational power, the algorithms marked as QCR are considered as resistant to such kind of computational power.

Short Key Lifetime

By reducing the lifetime of keys being used in connection, for example, from 24 hours to 30 minutes, the security level of legacy cyphers can be dramatically increased.

Elliptic Curve Cryptography (ECC)

Elliptic Curve Cryptography or ECC is used to create smaller cryptographic keys based on mathematical properties of elliptical curve, which makes it more efficient. Elliptic curves have applications in digital signatures, encryption, pseudo-random generators etc. ECC can also be used in conjunction with legacy public key encryption methods like RSA or DH. Some research shows that ECC can create the same level of security as of RSA or DH with small key size as compared to its predecessors. The following table shows the requirement of key size by RSA and ECC for implementing the same level of security.

RSA Key Size (bits)	ECC Key Size (bits)
1024	160
2048	224
3072	256
7680	384
15360	521

Table 3- Comparison of Key Size Between RSA and ECC

Cryptographic Concepts Mind Map

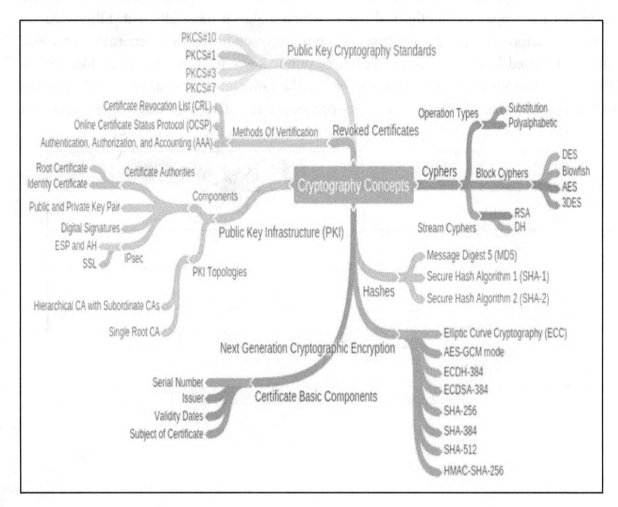

Figure 13- Cryptographic Concept's Mind Map

SSL DTL and TLS for Secure Communication

The terms SSL (Secure Socket Layer) and TLS (Transport Layer Security) are often used interchangeably, and provide encryption and authentication of data in motion. These protocols are intended to be used in a scenario where users want secure communication over unsecure network like public internet. Most common applications of such protocols are web browsing, Voice over IP (VOIP), and electronic mail.

Consider a scenario where a user wants to send an E-mail to someone or wants to purchase something from an online store where credit card credentials may be needed. SSL only spills the data after a process known as 'handshake'. If a hacker bypasses the encryption process than everything from bank account information to a secret conversation will be visible, which malicious users may use for personal gain.

SSL was developed by Netscape in 1994, with an intention to protect web transactions. The last version for SSL was version 3.0. In 1999, IETF created Transport Layer Security, which is also known as SSL 3.1 as TLS is in fact an adopted version of SSL.

Following are some of the most important functionalities SSL/TLS has been designed to do:

- Server authentication to client and vice versa
- Select common cryptographic algorithm
- Generate shared secrets between peers
- Protection of normal TCP/UDP connection

Working of SSL & TSL

The working of SSL and TSL is comprised of two phases:

Phase 1 (Session Establishment)

In this phase, common cryptographic protocol and peer authentication takes place. There are three sub-phases within overall phase 1 of SSL/TLS as explained below:

➢ **Sub-phase 1:** In this phase, "hello" messages are exchanged to negotiate common parameters of SSL/TLS for example, authentication and encryption algorithms

➢ **Sub-phase 2:** In this phase, one-way or two-way authentication is performed between client and server ends. A master key is sent from the client's side by using server's public key to start protecting the session

➢ **Sub-phase 3:** In the last phase, session key is calculated and cypher suite is finally activated. HMAC provides data integrity features by using either SHA-1 or MD5. Similarly, using DES-40, DES-CBC, 3DEC-EDE, 3DES-CBC, RC4-40, or RC4-128 will provide confidentiality features.

❖ **Session Keys Creation**

These are some of the methods, by which session keys are generated:

➢ *RSA Based.* Using public key of peer encrypts shared secret string.

➢ *A fixed DH Key Exchange.* Using fixed Diffie-Hellman based key being exchanged in a certificate will create session key

➢ *An ephemeral DH Key Exchange.* It is considered to be the best protection option as actual DH value will be signed with the private key of the sender and hence each session will have different set of keys

➢ *An anonymous DH Key Exchange without any Certificate or Signature.* Avoiding this option is advised, as it cannot prevent Man-in-the-Middle attacks

Phase 2 (Secure Data Transfer)

In this phase, secure data transfer takes place between encapsulating endpoints. Each SSL session has a unique session ID that is exchanged during authentication process. Session ID is used to differentiate between old and new session. The client can request server to resume the session based on this ID (if sever has that session ID in its cache).

TLS 1.0 is considered to be a bit more secure than last version of SSL (SSL v3.0). Even US Government has also declared not to use SSL v3.0 for highly sensitive communications, due to latest vulnerability named as POODLE. After POODLE vulnerability, most web browsers have disabled SSL v3.0 for maximum of the communications and services. Current browsers (Google Chrome, Firefox etc.) support TLS 1.0 by default and latest versions of TLS (TLS 1.1 and TLS 1.2) optionally. TLS 1.0 is considered to be equivalent of SSL3.0. However, newer versions of TLS are considered to be far more secure than SSL. It should be kept in mind that SSL v3.0 and TLS 1.0 is not compatible with each other as TLS uses Diffie-Hellman and Data Security Standard (DSS), while SSL uses RSA.

Apart from secure web browsing by using HTTPS, SSL/TLS can also be used for securing other protocols like FTP, SMTP and SNTP etc.

IPSec

IPSec stands for IP security. As the name suggests, it is used for the security of general IP traffic. The power of IPsec lies in its ability to support multiple protocols and algorithms. It also incorporates new advancements in encryption and hashing protocols. The main objective of IPSec is to provide CIA (Confidentiality, Integrity and Authentication) for virtual networks used in current networking environments. IPSec makes sure that the above objectives are in action by the time packet enters a VPN tunnel until the time it reaches the other end of the tunnel.

These are the key components that IPSec uses to provide the *CIA*:

➤ **Confidentiality**- IPSec uses encryption protocols namely AES, DES, and 3DES for providing confidentiality

➤ **Integrity**- IPSec uses hashing protocols (MD5 and SHA) for providing integrity. Hashed Message Authentication (HMAC) can also be used for checking the integrity of data

➤ **Authentication Algorithms**- RSA digital signatures and Pre-Shared Keys (PSKs) are two methods used for authentication purposes

Three protocols are used in IPSec to provide secure key exchange along with above defined features, namely:

- **IKEv1 or IKEv2**- Used for exchanging parameters utilized for key negotiation and overall establishment of Security Association (SA)

- **Encapsulation Security Payload (ESP)**- RFC 4303 Encapsulating Security Payload (ESP) provides framework for Data Encryption, Integrity, Authentication and anti-replay functionality of IPSec VPN using IPv4 and IPv6. It adds a new header and trailer field in the packet. ESP ensures the Confidentiality and Integrity of the packet payload by encrypting the payload, whereas using AH alone provides Integrity only. ESP header is placed in between IP header and Upper layer protocol header in a tunnel mode, whereas placed before encapsulated IP header in tunnel mode

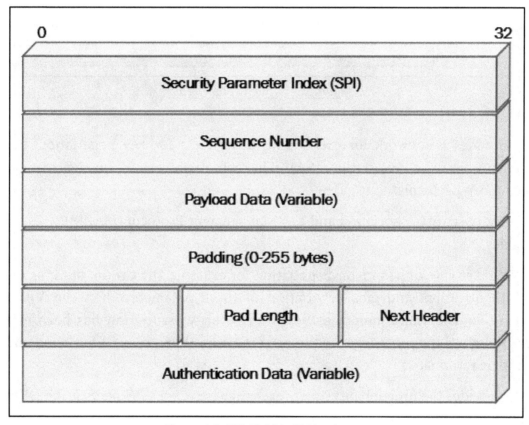

Figure 14- ESP Field in IP Header

- **Authentication Header (AH):** This provides framework for Data Authentication, Integrity and anti-reply functions. No encryption is provided in AH that is why ESP is preferred in most scenarios. RFC 4302 IP Authentication Header (AH) ensures the connectionless Integrity and the Authentication of data origin for each IP datagram. By this way, it also provides the protection against replay attacks. Authentication Header is not capable to encrypt the data hence it does not provide confidentiality, however it can be used as a standalone or combined with Encapsulating Security Payload (ESP).

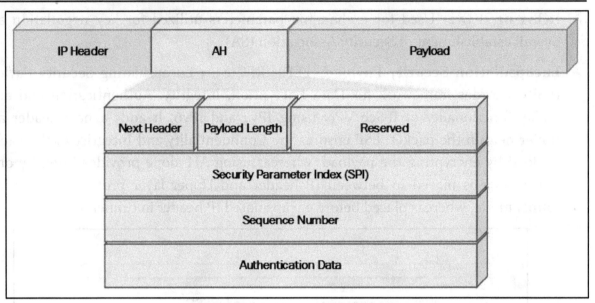

Figure 15- Authentication Header

IKEv1

IKEv1 provides framework for exchanging parameters for key negotiation and overall building of Security Association (SA). The actual process is further carried out by following two protocols:

- Internet Security Association and Key Management Protocol (ISAKMP)
- Oakley

ISAKMP takes care of parameter negotiation for example DH Group, lifetime, encryption and authentication, and etc. Negotiation of these parameters between VPN peers is necessary for the establishment of SA. After security association has been established, ISAKMP defines the procedure for the correct removal process of SA when connection is going to be terminated.

Oakley provides the functionality of key exchange between VPN peers using DH protocol. The DH protocol is asynchronous in nature, which means that each peer uses its own set of keys that are never shared with each other. Such kind of communication is considered to be much more secure than synchronous protocols like DES, 3DES etc. After the shared communication path has been established, both peers become ready to exchange the keys, which can be used by synchronous protocols for data encryption and hashing purposes.

The process of IKEv1 involves two steps. Both peers must go through the steps for the communication channel to be successfully established and a secure data flow may start as a result of it.

Step 1: IKE Phase 1 Negotiation Tunnel

The first step of initiation of VPN between two peers is known as IKE phase 1 tunnel. This phase is not used for sending encrypted user traffic. Instead, it is used for securing the management traffic related to VPN connection between two peers. For example, keeping alive packets to verify the status of VPN connection, PSK key or digital certificate for authentication between peers and encryption. Hashing algorithms used to protect this key or certificate are defined in IKE phase 1 tunnel. IKE phase 1 is called bidirectional because only one session key is used to encrypt both incoming and outgoing traffic.

Two modes, which can be used to define this tunnel namely are:

➤ **Main Mode-** Main mode uses more packets and as a result, processing power is more than the aggressive mode. Six different messages (three pair of messages) are exchanged between negotiating peers in main mode:

- First pair consists of IKEv1 security policies configure on device. One of the peer (initiator) starts sending one or more IKEv1 policies, and the other peer (responder) responds with its choice from the policies

- Second pair includes DH public key exchange. DH creates a shared key as per DH group being exchanged in first pair and then encrypts a random number, which is then exchanged between VPN peers

- Third pair is used for ISAKMP authentication. Each pair authenticates their validity by using either pre-shared key or digital certificate

➤ **Aggressive Mode-** Main goal of aggressive mode is same as main mode. Instead of six, this type for IKE phase 1 tunnel negotiation uses three messages. The overall process involves the following steps:

- The initiator sends randomly generated number being signed by DH group, IKEv1 policies and so on

- The other peer (responder) authenticates the packet and sends back accepted IKEv1 policies, nonce (the randomly generate number signed by DH group) and identification hash so that exchange gets completed

- The initiator authenticates the receiving packets and sends identification hash to the responder

There are five things that must be matched on both devices for *IKE phase 1 tunnel* to succeed:

- ➢ **Hashing Algorithm-** Message Digest (MD5) and Secure Hashing Algorithm (SHA) is commonly used in latest implementations

- ➢ **Encryption Algorithm-** Advanced Encryption Standard (AES), Digital Encryption Standard (DES) or 3DES is used for securing the key and management information used in phase 1. Longer key is preferred, as the longer it is, the more difficult it is to break

- ➢ **Diffie-Hellman (DH) Group-** It is used to generate symmetrical keys, which may be used by VPN peers for using symmetrical algorithms like *AES*. DH group number refers to the size of key (in bits) used to generate the above-mentioned key pair. Group 1 uses 768 bits; Group 2 uses 1024 bits while Group 5 uses 1536 bits. DH key exchange itself is asymmetrical in nature but the key it generates is symmetrical

- ➢ **Authentication Method-** It is used to verify the authenticity of VPN peers. Two options available are *Pre-Shared Keys (PSKs)* and *RSA Signatures* (Certificate based authentication)

- ➢ **Lifetime-** As the name suggests, it defines the time, after which IKE phase 1 tunnel will be teared down if it remains idle. Default lifetime is 3600 seconds (equal to one day). Normally, a smaller life is desired because a new DH key pair will be generated for each session, which gives an attacker a minor time space to calculate key pair used for current session before it times out

Step 2: IKE Phase 2 Tunnel

Authentication and hashing, as defined in the previous process, confuse most people as the main algorithms to be used secure end users IP traffic. However, the above-defined components are used only to secure the management communication between VPN peers. After successful establishment of IKE phase 1 tunnel, a second tunnel known as IKE phase 2 tunnel is established, again with mutual agreement, to secure the end user IP traffic.

This second mandatory phase uses the parameters being negotiated in phase 1 for secure IPSec SA creation. Unlike phase 1 SA, phase 2 IPSec SA are unidirectional, i.e. a different session key is used for traffic in each direction. Regardless of parameters selected within IKEv1 transform sets, the following pieces of information are always sent:

- IPSec Encryption Algorithm (Options: DES, 3DES, AES)
- IPSec Authentication Algorithm (Options: MD5, SHA-1)
- IPSec Protocol (AH or ESP)

- IPSec SA Lifetime (seconds or kilobytes)
- IPSec Mode of Operation (Transport or Tunnel).

IPSec Transforms

An IPSec transform specifies a single IPSec security protocol (either AH or ESP) with its corresponding security algorithms and mode. Some examples include the following:

➢ The **AH protocol** with the HMAC with MD5 authentication algorithm in tunnel mode is used for authentication. AH provides authentication mechanism for both data and IP header for packets by using one-way hash. One of the reasons ESP is preferred over AH is due to its support of encryption in ESP

➢ The **ESP protocol** with the triple DES (3DES) encryption algorithm in transport mode is used for confidentiality of data. ESP also provides integrity but not as granular as AH, which provides authentication of data and IP header as well

➢ The ESP protocol with the 56-bit DES encryption algorithm and the HMAC with SHA-1 authentication algorithm in tunnel mode are used for authentication and confidentiality

➢ Both ESP and AH operate at the network layer of OSI model and have their own protocol numbers (50 and 51 respectively)

➢ As AH functionality is absent in ASA, ESP will be used whenever ASA happens to be one of the peers of VPN

Transform Sets

A transform set is a combination of individual IPSec transforms designed to enact a specific security policy for traffic. During the ISAKMP IPSec security association negotiation that occurs in IKE phase 2 quick mode, the peers agree to use a particular transform set for protecting a particular data flow. Transform sets combine the following IPSec factors:

- Mechanism for payload authentication—AH transform
- Mechanism for payload encryption—ESP transform
- IPSec mode (transport versus tunnel)

Transform sets equal a combination of an AH transform, plus an ESP transform, plus the IPSec mode (either tunnel or transport mode)

IPSec Working Modes

There are two working modes of IPSec namely *tunnel* and *transport mode*. Each has its own features and implementation procedure.

IPSec Tunnel Mode: Being the default mode set in Cisco devices, tunnel mode protects the entire IP packet from the originating device. It means for every original packet, another packet is generated with new IP header and sent over the untrusted network to the VPN peer located on other end of logical connection. Tunnel mode is commonly used in case of Site-to-Site VPN where two secure IPSec gateways are connected over public internet using IPSec VPN connection. Consider the following diagram:

This shows IPSec Tunnel Mode with ESP header:

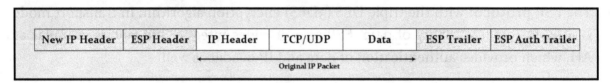

Figure 16- IPSec Tunnel Mode with ESP Header

Similarly, when AH is used, then the new IP Packet format will be:

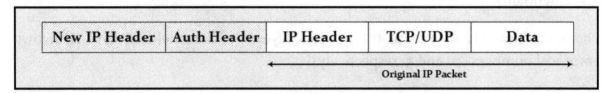

Figure 17- IPSec Tunnel Mode with AH Header

IPSec Transport Mode: In transport mode, IPSec VPN secures the data field or payload of originating IP traffic by using encryption, hashing or both. New IPSec headers encapsulate only payload field while the original IP headers remain unchanged. Tunnel mode is used when original IP packets are source and destination addresses of secure IPSec peers. For example, securing the management traffic of router is a perfect example of IPSec VPN implementation using transport mode. From configuration point of view, both tunnel and transport modes are defined in configuration of *transform set*. It will be covered in the Lab scenario of this section.

This diagram shows IPSec Transport Mode with ESP header:

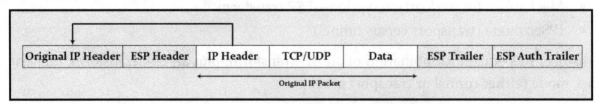

Figure 18- IPSec Transport Mode with ESP Header

Similarly, in case of AH:

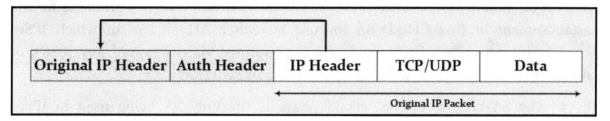

Figure 19- IPSec Transport Mode with AH Header

IKEv2

The original IKEv1 protocol proves to be a reliable security framework for many years and was used in majority deployments of site-to-site and remote access VPN solutions. The Cisco IPSec VPN client software supports IKEv1 for establishing IPSec based remote access connection. However, difficulties were faced due to complexity of IKEv1 and no support for different extensions, which are considered to be essential for remote access clients (for example, NAT-T etc.). As a result of this, every vendor implemented their own versions of required features, although different standards were created later on for different extensions like NAT-T and remote address acquisition etc.

Both IKEv1 and IKEv2 use UDP port number 500 for encapsulation and information transfer between peers. Despite of header format similarity, both protocols do not interoperate with each other.

As IKEv2 (RFC 5996) was created to simplify as well as streamline the processes and architecture of IKEv1, it combines the contents of IKE (RFC 2409), ISAKMP (RFC 2408), Internet Domain of Interpretation (RFC 2407), NAT-T, legacy authentication and remote access acquisition.

IKEv1 uses either nine messages (6 for Main Mode and 3 for Quick Mode) or six messages (3 for Aggressive Mode and 3 for Quick Mode) for successful creation of IKE and IPSec SAs for secure communication tunnel. IKEv2 replaces this legacy method with new process which involves exchange of just four messages instead of nine or six.

These are the new exchange types that replace Main Mode, Aggressive Mode, or Quick Mode of IKEv1:

➢ **KE_SA_INIT (Phase 1)**- In the first exchange, security parameters in the form of IKEv2 proposals are negotiated between both peers, which may include integrity and encryption protocols, DH values, and nonce (random numbers). The seed security key value, also known as SKEYSEED, is also created in this phase. All future IKE Keys are also generated from SKEYSEED. The messages in remaining process are also encrypted and authenticated by using keys that are also generated from SKEYSEED

➤ **IKE_AUTH (Phase 1 and 2)**- The second phase is used for validation of peers' identity and negotiation of various encryption, authentication, and integrity protocols for the establishment of first CHILD_SA for use by either AH or ESP in which IPSec communication occurs. Peers validation is performed via Pre-Shared Key (PSK), or digital certificates or Extensible Authentication Protocol (EAP)

- The SA created in the second phase is the only SA being used in IPSec communication in IKEv2. However, depending on application or peer's requirement, IKEv2 uses CREATE_SA_CHILD exchange. During CREATE_SA_CHILD exchange, new DH values may be created along with the usage of new cryptographic protocols

- IKEv2 can also have fourth exchange type known as INFORMATIONAL to exchange error as well as management information between peers

- As far as simplicity is concerned, most of the extensions for example, NAT-T is built-in within IKEv2. Similarly, keep alive functionality between peers, allows IKEv2 to recognize when tunnel is down and regeneration of tunnel is required. VPN overload is also reduced in case of IKEv2. For example, IKEv2 creates a single SA for multiple networks and subnets while IKEv1 creates a separate SA for each source and destination subnet/network

Site-to-Site VPN Solutions

With the evolution of Internet and the increasing interest of businesses becoming IP enabled, Site-to-Site VPN solutions from Cisco help organizations to quickly establish secure and encrypted communication channels with business partners and remote offices with dramatically lower cost than physical dedicated lines. One of the advantages of using Site-to-Site VPN solutions is that end user remains unaware of underlying technology as no configuration needs to be done on client side.

Categories of Site-to-Site VPN Solutions

Generally, there are four major categories of VPN topologies, which are used to create Site to Site VPN:

➤ **Point-to-Point VPN Connection**- An example of this would be two sites HQ and Branch office using secure VPN connection. Both sites' devices require manual creation of VPN connection

➤ **Hub and Spoke Network**- The central site known as Hub has major configuration of VPN connection while remote sites known as Spoke, only has information of how to securely connect to Hub. Traffic from one Spoke to another Spoke is relayed via Hub

> **Partially Meshed Network**- Most of the sites have VPN connections with each other. New VPN connection may be built as per requirement

> **Fully Meshed Network**- Provides most optimal traffic flow as each site has VPN connection with every other site

VPN Technology Consideration

Guidelines for Choosing VPN LAN Topology

The general guidelines that should be kept in mind when deciding which VPN topology provide best performance for the given network are as follows:

- Standard IP Sec Site-to-Site connection must be used when number of sites is to be securely connected; it is low and their management is manageable

- Use Hub and Spoke based VPN connectivity if underlying network architecture is already in similar fashion. It will result in easier implementation and management of VPN topology

- Full Mesh VPN connectivity must be implemented when any-to-any connection is required along with optimal traffic flow

Guidelines for Choosing VPN WAN Topology

These are the general guidelines that should be kept in mind when deciding which VPN topology should depend on WAN infrastructure:

> **Transport Network Routing**- Determines whether tunnelling or non-tunnelling based VPN technology will be suitable for current scenario

> **Topology**- Identifying which topology will suit the current network scenario based on different authentication and configuration methods

The main Site-to-Site VPN WAN technologies being available in Cisco IOS are:

> **Individual IPSec Tunnels**- In this technology, Virtual Tunnel Interfaces (VTIs) or GRE over IPSec Tunnels are created for every point-to-point connection, which makes it a very low scalable solution. If Pre-Shared Keys (PSKs) are used for authentication between peers, then this solution may also be considered to have low scalability in terms of authentication

> ➢ **Cisco Easy VPN**- It can be used in Hub and Spoke environments as Easy VPN has a very high authentication and configuration scalability as most of the configuration part is done on Hub

> ➢ **Cisco DMVPN**- Like Easy VPN, DMVPN also works in Hub and Spoke based environments by allowing automatic creation of tunnels for communication between Spoke-to-Spoke. DMVPN can be implemented in Hub and Spoke, partial mesh and full mesh environments

> ➢ **Cisco GETVPN**- GET VPN is highly suitable in MPLS based network environment as it retains the original IP headers. GETVPN uses the concept Key Servers that makes it highly scalable in terms of configuration and authentication

This table summarizes the features of above four VPN technologies:

Feature	P2P IPSec	Easy VPN	DMVPN	GET VPN
Encapsulation	Tunnelled IPSec	Tunnelled IPSec	Tunnelled IPSec	Non-tunnelled IPSec
Configuration Scalability	Low	High for Hub	High for any device	High for any device
Authentication Scalability	Low	High with PSK/PKI	High with PKI	High with PSK/PKI
Suitable Topologies	P2P	Hub/Spoke	Hub/Spoke Partial Mesh Full Mesh	Full Mesh
Suitable Transport Networks	Any	Any	Any	Private WAN, MPLS

Table 4- Site-to-Site VPNs Comparison

In this section, various Site-to-Site VPN technologies will be discussed followed by the best-case scenario for each type.

Dynamic Multipoint VPN (DMVPN)

As the Site-to-Site VPN solution is primarily used for connecting main office with multiple branch offices for unique IP subnet, the configuration for network administrator gets complex as number of branch offices increases. By defining static configurations like crypto-maps and pre-shared keys on each device, maintaining such network topology becomes a full time job as well.

In such situations, DMVPN comes to the rescue by providing same output while keeping low cost, less configuration complexity and increasing flexibility of the overall network design.

In DMVPN, one device acts as central part of whole VPN topology while the remaining ones act as client to the central device for fetching information regarding VPN connection and destination address for intended connections. The central device is known as HUB, while remaining devices are called SPOKE. Normally, headquarter edge device is configured as HUB, while branch offices' device is configured as SPOKE.

Deployment of DMVPN consists of two main design considerations:

➤ **DMVPN Hub and Spoke**- Used for interconnecting headquarter with branch office. In this mode of deployment, traffic between branch offices flow through hub as there is not direct communication between different Spokes

➤ **DMVPN Spoke-to-Spoke**- Used for branch-to-branch direct communication. It should be noted that Hub-and-Spoke topology is initially generated. Full or partial mesh network will be created once traffic from one Spoke to some other Spoke is generated

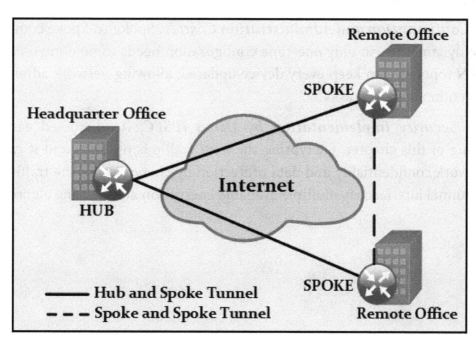

Figure 20- DMVPN Design Overview

From the diagram, only one interface needs to be created on Hub device, while each Spoke device will connect to this interface that is kind of shared with each branch office device. Static IP will always be assigned to Hub interface while Spoke device's interface can have static or dynamic IP address assignment.

As discussed earlier, DMVPN has cleaner and less complex configurations than Standard Site-to-Site VPN. This benefit of DMVPN is just because of this shared interface known as multiple GRE (mGRE) tunnel.

mGRE tunnel interface along with Next Hop Resolution Protocol (NHRP) help Spoke devices to communicate with Hub or any other Spoke. NHRP is a layer 2 protocol and works exactly like Address Resolution Protocol (ARP). The Hub device holds special database known as NHRP database and contains the public IP addresses of configured Spoke. Whenever a Spoke wants communication with some other Spoke, it queries the NHRP database from Hub for intended public IP address.

Benefits of using DMVPN

The most prominent benefits of DMVPN that makes it popular and recommended solution for Site-to-Site VPN implementation are as follows:

➢ **Simplified Hub Configuration:** Unlike standard Site-to-Site VPN solution, only one tunnel interface (mGRE) needs to be created. No matter how many Spoke device there are, the Hub configuration remains the same

➢ **Dynamic IP Addressing Support for Spoke Devices**: As Spoke devices use NHRP protocol to make communication with other Spokes, it is not mandatory to have static IP address on Spoke devices

➢ **Lower Configuration and Administration Cost:** As Spoke-to-Spoke communication is done dynamically, so only one-time configuration needs to be done on each device and VPN topology can keep every device updated, allowing network administrator to focus on other complex tasks

➢ **Option Security Implementation by Using IPSEC**: As discussed earlier at the beginning of this chapter, encrypting the VPN traffic is optional and it can enhance the network confidentiality and data protection by encryption of the traffic traversing mGRE tunnel interface via multiple available encryption and hashing algorithms

DMVPN Deployment Models

The most commonly found DMVPN deployment models found in different network topologies around the globe are:

> ➤ Single DMVPN Network - Single Tier Headend Architecture

> ➤ Single DMVPN Network - Dual Tier Headend Architecture

> ➤ Dual DMVPN Network– Single Tier Headend Architecture

> ➤ Dual DMVPN Network– Dual Tier Headend Architecture

Independent from which model is implemented, DMVPN creation always involves the following components or control planes:

> ➤ mGRE tunnels

> ➤ Next Hop Resolution Protocol based dynamic routing

> ➤ IPSec based mGRE tunnel protection

Single DMVPN Network - Single Tier Headend Architecture

The simplest implementation of DMVPN is by using single Hub device and connecting Spoke devices to it, as shown below:

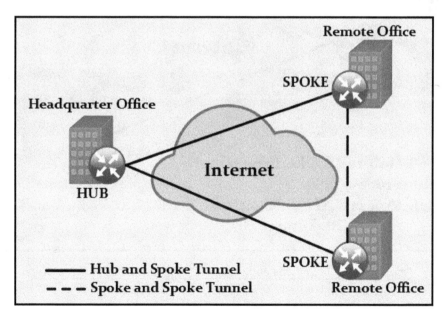

Figure 21- Single DMVPN Network Design

By Single Tier Headend, it means that every single component will be performed and controlled via a single Hub device. The central device, i.e. HUB maintains NHRP database to be aware of every Spoke in VPN topology.

During the initial configuration, each Spoke gets configured with static NHRP mapping and it dynamically knows every other Spoke device in the VPN network.

The Single DMVPN-Single Tier Headend architecture is suitable for limited budget DMVPN deployment as Hub acts a single point of failure in the whole design. If the internet or mGRE tunnel interface gets down due to any reason, it will tear down the whole VPN network.

Single DMVPN Network - Dual Tier Headend Architecture

In the previous design, the CPU processing limitation of single HUB device also poses a serious threat to overall VPN network. In order to facilitate the DMVPN topology, a dual tier headend design is used in which control planes or DMVPN components are performed mutually between two devices that are shown below:

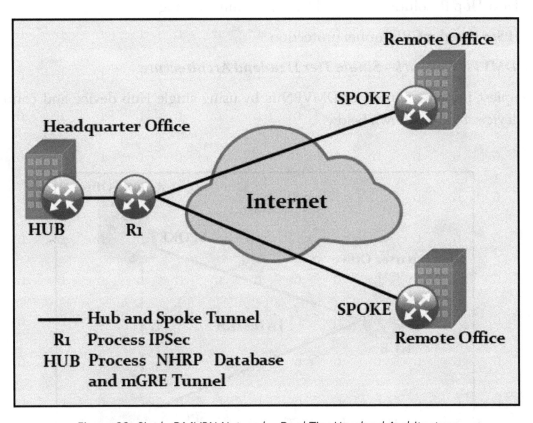

Figure 22- Single DMVPN Network - Dual Tier Headend Architecture

Apart from the distribution of processing tasks, the only real advantage of using this design is support for large number of Spokes. Such design also has a limitation of not supporting Spoke-to-Spoke communication directly.

Dual DMVPN Network– Single Tier Headend Architecture

One of the most critical errors stated in the previous designs is the single point of failure in case Hub gets down. To cater to such problems, Two Hubs with two independent DMVPN networks can be established. Each Hub will process its own control planes. Similarly Spoke-to-Spoke communication will be done via respective tunnels of each DMVPN network. For auto failover mechanism, a dynamic routing protocol like EIGRP or OSPF needs to be enabled so that if HUB1 gets down the secondary DMVPN network (HUB2) takes over.

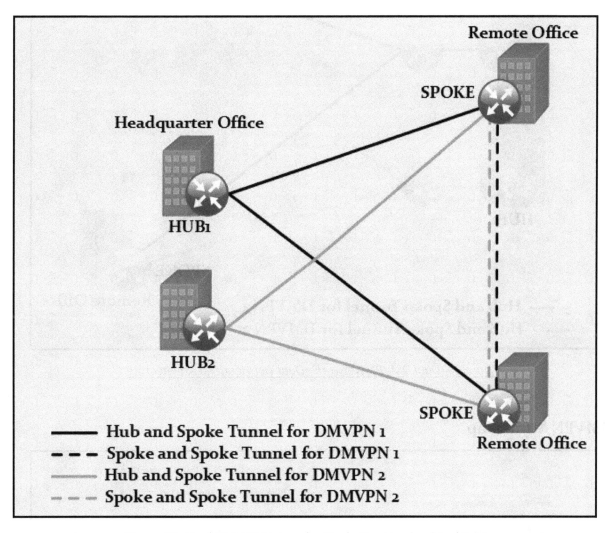

Figure 23- Dual DMVPN Network– Single Tier Headend Architecture

Dual DMVPN Network– Dual Tier Headend Architecture

In order to relieve the HUB1 and HUB2 routers with some of their duties as shown above, Dual Tier Headend design introduces two frontend routers to perform encryption while HUB1 and HUB2 maintain respective NHRP database and mGRE tunnels. In order to

make sure auto failover capability of DMVPN network, dynamic routing protocol (EIGRP or OSPF) needs to be enabled over DMVPN network.

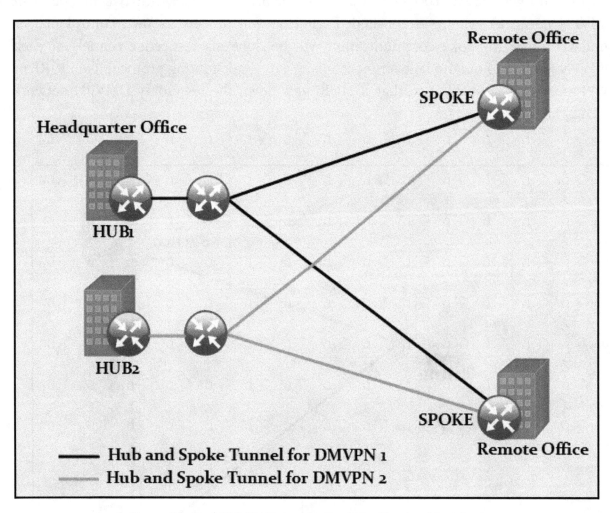

Figure 24- Dual DMVPN Network– Dual Tier Headend Architecture

DMVPN Mind Map

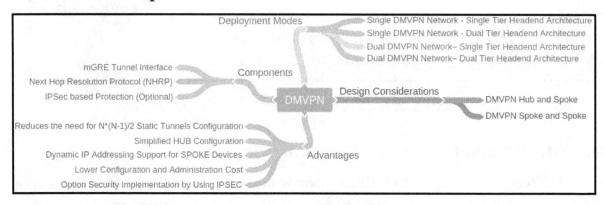

Figure 25- DMVPN Mind Map

Flex VPN

In the previously discussed VPN technologies, only configuration style was minimally changed, and overall, it remains the same. In Cisco IOS based platforms, the following are few technologies by which Site-to-Site VPN connections can be achieved:

Crypto Maps

Using static configuration like hashing and encryption algorithms on both VPN gateways is one of the legacy methods of implementing Site-to-Site VPN connections. However, it is still effective in case of vendor interoperability.

VTI

Logical interfaces are defined and are used in IPSec implementations, hence eliminating the need to define Generic Routing Encapsulation (GRE) tunnels.

Easy VPN

Simplifies the VPN connection by making branch devices as clients to the Easy VPN server (also known as VPN Concentrator). Just like DMVPN, Easy VPN client gets attributes or policy from Server device, which greatly increases the flexibility of overall design.

DMVPN

Provides better flexibility and scalability option by dynamic creation of tunnels between Spoke-to-Hub and Spoke-to-Spoke communication by using mGRE tunnel and NHRP Protocol.

In order to merge multiple technologies, Cisco has introduced Flex VPN. As the name suggests, Flex VPN is flexible enough to entertain multiple technologies of Site-to-Site VPN technologies. These are the few possibilities:

- Device implementing Flex VPN can be configured to entertain connections from above defined technologies

- Flex VPN supports remote access by Cisco AnyConnect clients as well as Windows 7 native clients

- Flex VPN supports both IPV4 and IPV6 addressing based implementations

- Authentication/Authorization may be performed via local database or server based (like RADIUS etc.)

Apart from these possibilities, Flex VPN also has a down side of not supporting IKEv1. Flex VPN only supports IKEv2 (explained in the coming section). Although IKEV2 is not

backward compatible with IKEv1, it offers enhanced security features by supporting Next Generation Encryption Algorithms.

Group Encrypted Transport VPN(GETVPN)

Previously discussed VPN technologies like DMVPN uses secure tunnels based approach between Hub-to-Spoke and Spoke-to-Spoke communication. In GET VPN, IPSec is used for encryption but group Security Association (SA) is used instead of traditional LAN-to-LAN tunnel based approach.

Similarly, in traditional DMVN, a secondary routing domain is required for networks running over the logical tunnels. GETVPN can use the underlying network, hence traditional problems being faced in point-to-point IPSec tunnels are already solved in GETVPN as it is tunnel-less. Every device in a certain group known as Group Member (GM), can encrypt and decrypt the traffic as per Group Security Association (SA) profile.

Components of GETVPN

The following are the main components of GETVPN:

- Group Domain of Interpretation (GDOI)
- Key Servers (KSs)
- Cooperative KSs
- Group Members (GMs)
- IP Tunnel Header Preservation
- Group Security Association (SA)
- Rekey Mechanism
- Time-Based Anti Replay (TBAR)

Group Domain of Interpretation (GDOI)

Being one of the key components of GETVPN, GDOI key management protocol distributes IPSec keys and common policies to VPN Gateways (Group Members or GM). Rekey mechanism refreshes these keys periodically. GDOI is an extension of IKE/ISAKMP and uses UDP port number 848.

GDOI protocol is protected by IKE phase 1 negotiations. The participating VPN gateways authenticate themselves with the device providing the IPSec Keys and common group policies via Pre-Shared Key (PSK) or Public Key Infrastructure (PKI). After devices get authenticated, IKE process expires and GDOI protocol is then used to update Group members in a more protected and scalable manner.

GDOI uses two types of keys for encryption. The key used for encrypting control plan is Key Encryption Key (KEK) and for data plane traffic encryption, Traffic Encryption Key (TEK) is used.

IP Tunnel Header Preservation

Just like IPSec Transport mode, GETVPN retains the original IP header, but one of the problems with IPSec Transport mode is the reassembly and the fragmentation of packets.

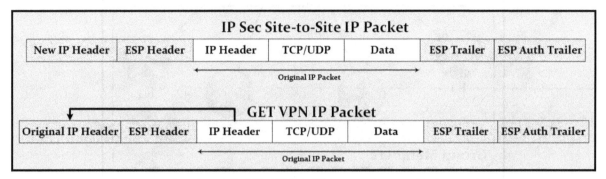

Figure 26- GETVPN IP Packet Structure

GETVPN is suitable for MPLS (L2 and L3) infrastructure, where VPN gateways have end-to-end IP connectivity. As private IP addressing scheme is not supported in public internet cloud, NAT interferes with IP header preservation. GETVPN can be used in conjunction with DMVPN, where DMVPN provides routing and GETVPN is used for encryption purposes.

Key Servers

One of the most important components in GETVPN technology is Key Server or KS. KS is responsible for pushing the common SA/encryption policies, interested traffic for encryption and rekey timers etc. to GMs. This implies that major configuration needs to be done on KS.

As Access Control List (ACL) is used on KS to define the intended traffic for encryption, which is downloaded by every other GM, it is always advised to use symmetric and summarized Access-List Entries (ACEs) to make ACL simple and short. "Permit IP ANY ANY" can also be used in ACL but routing protocol, PIM and other relevant traffic must be denied first.

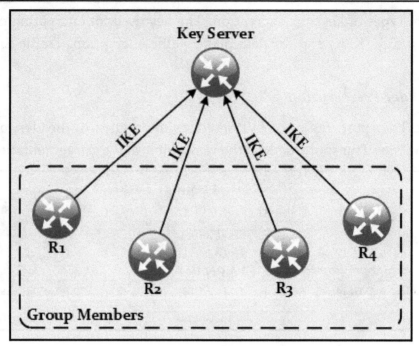

Figure 27- KS and GMs of GETVPN

A device acting as Key Server (KS) cannot be a Group Member at a time.

Group Members (GM)

GM is the actual device performing encryption/decryption of data traffic. The GM requires only IKE phase 1 parameters to be defined locally for authentication with KS. It will fetch the remaining configuration from Key Server (KS). Local Policy can also be defined on GM to be used for encryption and decryption.

Group Security Association (SA)

GETVPN uses the concept of SA for communication between GMs for common encryption policies and keys. As there is no need for IPSec negotiations in this case, hence it reduces the workload on GMs.

Rekey Mechanism

The actual keys are sent to every GM by Key Server (KS). If a GM does not get rekey information from KS, it will try to register again with KS. If successful, it will receive the SA information as regular process, otherwise the current IPSec SA will expire and as a result, data flow will be stopped.

The Rekey Process can be unicast or multicast. If key is sent via unicast message to GMs, then ACK is expected from every GM. If an ACK is not received for three consecutive tries by KS, then respective GM is removed from a list on KS and will not be sent to that specific GM by next transmission. The number of retransmission attempts and their interval is configurable like any other routing protocol.

If key is sent via multicast, then ACK is not expected from GMs. Every GM joins the multicast group at the time of registration with Key Server. As only single message is sent via KS which is then sent to every multicast group member, and CPU workload is a lot less as compared to unicast procedure.

Cooperative KSs

As Key Server is key to the proper working of GET VPN, there should be multiple KSs in case primary one gets down due to any reason. The GMs are added to the list of KSs. Election is held on boot up process of GETVPN, where the KS with highest configured priority takes the role of primary KS. Maximum of 8 Key Servers are allowed on a network and election process is carried out via proprietary protocol known as Cooperative Key Server Protocol (COOP).

The GMs can register to any KS but only primary KS has the ability to send rekey messages. The Cooperative KSs exchange announcement messages primary to secondary KSs. If secondary KS does not hear from primary KS, it contacts the primary KS. In case secondary KS does not get a reply from primary one, an election will be triggered and new primary KS will be elected.

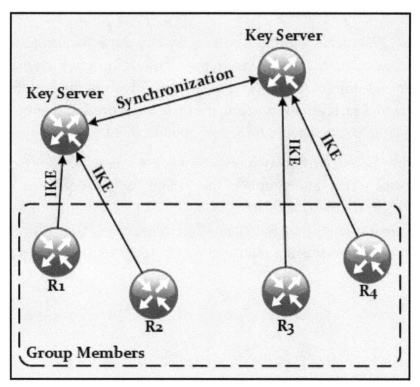

Figure 28- Redundant Key Servers

The announcement messages from Primary KS may contain:

- ➢ **Sender Priority**- Defines the priority of sender. As explained earlier, KS with higher priority will take the role of Primary KS. If two KSs have the same value, then the device with highest IP address wins the election process

- ➢ **Maintaining the Sender Role**- It is quite possible that KS may be distributed geographically at larger distances that may result in network latency and delay issues. As a result of slow synchronization, multiple KSs may become Primary KS, which will revert to original roles after message exchange and synchronization

- ➢ **Request for Return Packet Flag**- As these announcement messages are one way, a KS can also request the state information from peer devices to find out its role

- ➢ **Group State**- This contains the current IPSec SA and respective keys being valid for specific groups

  Use of multiple Key Servers has following advantages:

  - Allows GM to register with closest KS for performance reasons

  - Key Server redundancy is required as major workload of GETVPN is done by KS

Time-Based Anti Replay (TBAR)

Traditional IPSec VPN technologies use anti replay based mechanism to mitigate attacks, in which an attacker actually sniffs the encrypted data traffic and then uses it to generate attacks on IPSec end-points. Anti-replay mechanism involves the counter based sliding window, in which the receiver always compares the sequence number of received packet to determine whether packet should be accepted or dropped.

In GETVPN, a time based anti-replay mechanism is used, in which Key Server (KS) uses a pseudo time clock. This also implies that there is no need for Network Time Protocol(NTP). KS syncs the clock with all GMs of GETVPN domain. Every GM puts the pseudo clock as time stamp in the data packets. The receiving GM will compare this field with the global pseudo clock being managed by KS. If packet is received too late, then it will be dropped.

This table compares GETVPN with DMVPN:

Feature	DMPVN	GETVPN
Network Infrastructure	Public Interne Transport	Private IP Transport
Network Style	Hub-to-Spoke, Spoke-to-Spoke	Any-to-Any
Routing	Dynamic Routing on Tunnels	Dynamic Routing on IP WAN
Failover Redundancy	Route Distribution Model	Route Distribution Model and Stateful
Encryption Style	Peer-to-Peer Protection	Group Protection
IP Multicast	Multicast Replication at Hub	Multicast Replication in IP WAN Network

Table 5- GETVPN & DMVPN Comparison

Benefits and Limitations of GETVPN

These are the key benefits of using GETVPN:

- Very scalable in terms of adding new Group Members in a full mesh, as little configuration is required on GM
- Scalable support for multicast traffic

On the other hand, the main limitations of GETVPN are:

- Addressing scheme used in VPN topology must be routable in the transport network due to the fact that GETVPN retains the original IP header
- As session keys are shared between group of VPN gateways, single peer may have considerable impact if compromised
- Availability of Key Servers must be made sure as the whole concept of GETVPN is based on it

GETVPN Mind Map

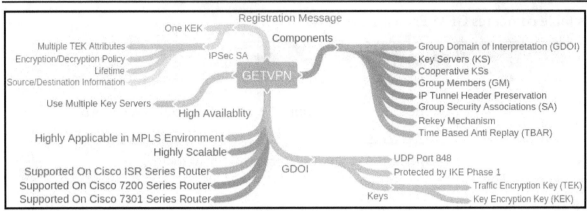

Figure 29- GETVPN Mind Map

High Availability Consideration for Site-to-Site VPN Solutions

Reverse Route Injection (RRI)

Reverse Route Injection (RRI) is the injection process of static routes automatically into the routing process of those networks/hosts, which are protected by remote tunnel endpoints. RRI distance Metric is used to configure the administrative distance of the static route having precedence over dynamic routes or setting up as backup route, used in the absence of dynamically learned route to the VPN device. The command set reverse-route distance is used in crypto map or IPsec profile to specify the distance metric of VPN routes.

Configuring RRI Under a Static Crypto Map
crypto map *map-name seq-name* **ipsec-isakmp** Creates or modifies a crypto map entry and enters crypto map configuration mode. **reverse-route** [**static** | **remote-peer** *ip-address* [**gateway**] [**static**]] Creates source proxy information for a crypto map entry. **set reverse-route** [**distance** *number* | **tag** *tag-id*] Specifies a distance metric to be used or a tag value to be associated with these routes.

Hot Standby Router Protocol (HSRP)

IPSec Stateful failover (VPN High Availability) is basically a feature that ensures the availability of VPN by overcoming the outage. Continuity of routing can be controlled by deployment of standby routers. These standby routers take control when the primary device goes down. As the process of standby router becomes active and continues the processing, it is transparent for local and remote users depending upon the HSRP timers configured. Hot Standby Routing Protocol (HSRP) is specially designed for ensuring the high availability in the networks by using standby router, which monitors the primary active router, when the primary active router goes down, it takes control, hence providing redundancy. HSRP and IPSec Stateful failover enable active router to send the following information to the standby router:

- IKE cookies stamp
- Session keys
- Cisco Service Assurance (SA) Agent attributes
- Sequence number counter and window state
- Kilobyte (KB) lifetime expirations
- Dead Peer Detection (DPD) sequence number updates

There are four possible configurations for High Availability Site-to-Site VPN Solutions:

1. Non-GRE High Availability (HA) with a virtual IP (VIP), on outside and inside interfaces:

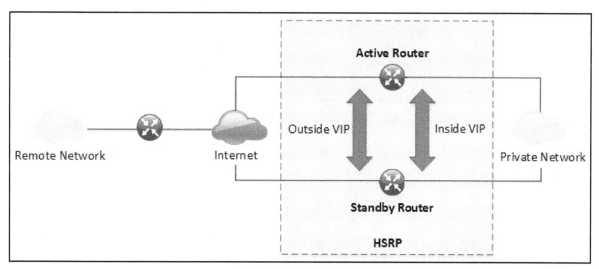

Figure 30- Non-GRE HA with VIP on Inside & Outside Interfaces

2. Non-GRE HA with only VIPs on the outside. The route to the outside is provided by Reverse Route Injection (RRI):

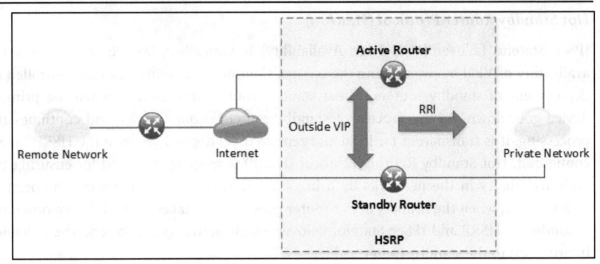

Figure 31- Non-GRE HA with VIP on Outside Interface only & RRI

3. GRE HA, with VIPs on the outside and inside Interfaces:

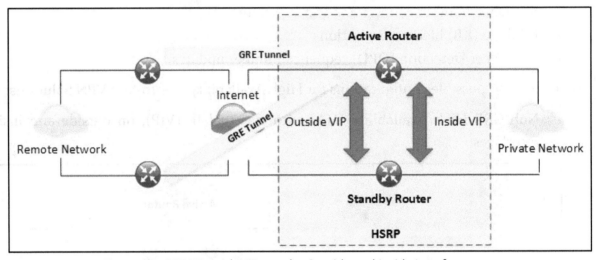

Figure 32- GRE HA, with VIPs on the Outside and Inside Interfaces

4. GRE HA, with only a VIP on the outside, using RRI:

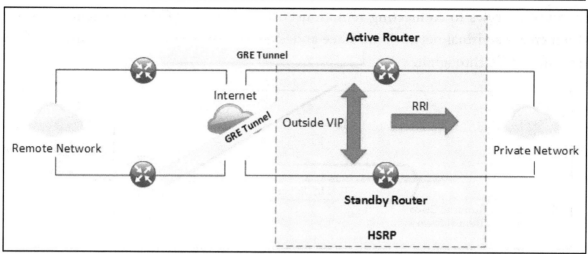

Figure 33- GRE HA with only a VIP on the Outside, Using RRI

Remote Access VPN Solutions

In the previous section of the workbook, different VPN solutions were discussed where whole office gets securely connected to branch or remote offices. However, there may be some scenarios where customers want to access official resources of organization's internal network from home or some café, in such cases remote access VPN comes really handy.

Remote Access(RA) VPNs uses very strong client authentication for users to prove their identity and strong encryption for secure communication. Some RA VPNs even go beyond encryption and authentication to perform some high level functionalities like checking the security posture of client before giving access and providing limited access of organization's resources.

The two primary methods, by which encapsulation for VPN deployment are SSL/TLS and IPSec based encapsulation protocols.

These are the major modes of encapsulating end-user traffic:

Full Tunnelling VPNs

Requires VPN client software (Cisco AnyConnect) to be installed on remote machine or hardware based VPN devices in order to have fully routed IP access to organization's internal resources. Cisco IOS software running on ISR series routers provides support for SSL VPNs and IPSec based Easy VPNs fully tunnelling software clients. The ISR router acts as VPN Gateway and remote user's session terminates here. Cisco ISR router can also act as EZVPN IPSec hardware client and provide VPN access to entire remote network. After successful authentication, VPN Gateway (ISR Router) applies authorization and

accounting rules to connecting remote user. The Cisco AnyConnect client software will then create a virtual network interface and SSL/TLS based tunnel will be used to forward specific traffic through it.

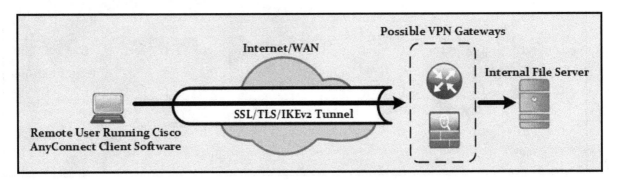

Figure 34- Cisco AnyConnect Client Software Diagram

This table lists the advantages and disadvantages of using full tunnelling VPNs:

Advantages	Disadvantages
No modification required for IP based applications	SSL VPN client needs to be installed on user machine
No end user's training required except for initiation and termination of VPN connection	Administrative privileges are required to install VPN client software
VPN encapsulation uses HTTPS (port 443) bypass Network Address Translation (NAT) and most firewalls just like any other HTTPS based session	
As VPN client software needs to be installed on end-machines, such kind of VPNs are mostly used on managed devices. They are considered to be more secure than unmanaged devices	

Table 6- Benefits and Limitations of Fully Tunnelling VPNs

Clientless VPN

Allows corporate users to access an organization's internal resources even when VPN client is not installed on remote machines. It requires users to open web browser that acts as VPN client and VPN Gateway acts as proxy to internal resources. This solution allows remote users to launch specific applications via web portal, for which they have been

granted access to. Clientless VPNs are easy to deploy then full tunnelling VPNs but provide limited access. Clientless VPN provides access to remote users with the following techniques:

- **URL and Common Internet File System (CIFS) File Access**- When a user is authenticated, a web page is presented containing pre-configured bookmarks. The user can access pre-configured web pages or file system from bookmarks

- **Port Forwarding**- Provides access to applications built on TCP ports by mapping application specific ports on remote machine to internal servers. Java applet needs to be installed on remote machine, which listens on remote machines' ports and forwards the connection to the VPN gateway

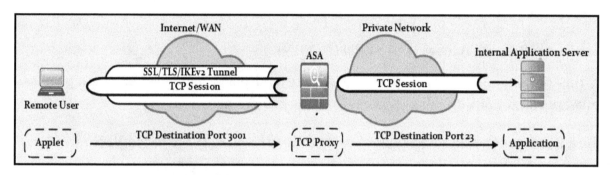

Figure 35- Port Forwarding Diagram

- **Client/Server Plugins**- Plugins enable users to access their familiar applications from within the web browser window. Unlike port forwarding, user can connect to VPN and access their specific application without any need for application to be locally installed. Available plugins are Remote Desktop Protocol (RDP), VNC, Secure Shell (SSH), Telnet, and Citrix

The advantages and disadvantages of using Clientless VPNs are:

Advantages	Disadvantages
As VPN encapsulation uses HTTPS (port 443) bypass Network Address Translation (NAT) and most firewalls just like any other HTTPS based session	Most of the web based client-server applications are supported by this kind of VPN
No installation of VPN software is required on remote machine	User training might be required as most of the users may not be used to such kind of resources access

As no installation is done on the remote machine, administrative privilege is not required for remote users	A layered security approach is required as any computer with web browser can perform a login attempt

Table 7- Benefits and Limitations of Clientless VPNs

Software Remote Access IPSec VPN (EZVPN)

With this option, remote users use Cisco VPN Client software to create an IPSec VPN tunnel with ISR router, which acts as a VPN gateway. Just like full tunnelling VPN, after mutual authentication, VPN gateway applies appropriate accounting and authorization policies on remote user's session. After policies are applied, remote user can send data through the IPSec tunnel.

Hardware Remote Access IPSec VPN (EZVPN)

In this option, Cisco device acts as a remote end-point, which after same process as software based EZPVPN, allows access to entire remote network.

The advantages and disadvantages of using fully tunnelling IPSec based VPNs are:

Advantages	Disadvantages
No modification required for any kind of IP based applications	Cisco VPN client software needs to be installed on remote machines
No end user's training required except for initiation and termination of VPN connection	Administrative privileges are required to install VPN client software
Support for real-time applications like IP voice and video streaming	By default, it cannot traverse firewall as IPSec, and IKE might not be allowed through it
As installation of IPSec VPN client is mandatory for this kind of VPN, it is typically used on managed devices	

Table 8- Benefits and Limitations of Full Tunnelling IPSec VPNs

Clientless SSL Browser & Client Consideration

As remote access VPN connects the remote endpoint to the corporate network, it also creates a risk of security of the entire network as it might be an entry point for the threat. Although Remote access VPN such as SSL VPN & its Clientless nature provide a significant benefit and mobility but require additional security as compared to other remote access VPN.

Security Threat

Clientless nature of SSL VPN supports remote users from public domain can be connected to the trusted private network. It is a major security risk as these public domain devices are not secure enough against threats. In a corporate network security & IT department ensures the installation of security software and anti-virus on each node to protect the device and network. If a remote user connects to the VPN network via a compromised PC, or an unsecured device, it can be a source of spreading malwares and viruses into the VPN network.

Downloads

Remotely connected VPN user may also download sensitive confidential files on an untrusted PC for any purpose such as working on it, reading, forwarding etc. These files can be left intentionally or unintentionally, however they can also be recovered from hard disk.

Browser Cache

As we know, while using internet, internet browsers store web pages and its objects into their cache to improve the performance and browsing. These cache files are stored on a directory of the running system. If a user connects to the VPN network from a system and browses anything, it will be stored in the cache file, located in the local directory, which can be accessed by another user.

History & Cookies

By accessing the browser's history, you can easily figure out what activities have been done so far on the internet browser. Remote VPN user may be using a device that is available for other users. Anyone can easily reveal the activities by accessing the browser history. Similarly, Cookies are stored, which can also reveal sensitive information of previously logged user.

AnyConnect Client Requirements

AnyConnect Certificate Requirements

1. SSL connections via FQDN do not perform Secondary server verification in initial verification via FQDN fails.

2. Server certificates in IPsec and SSL connections containing Key Usage require Digital Signature & KeyAgreement or KeyEncipherment attributes.

3. Server certificates in SSL connections containing EKU require serverAuth attribute.

4. Server certificates in IPSec connections containing EKU require serverAuth OR ikeIntermediate attribute.

5. IPsec connections perform name verification on server certificates

- In the presence of Subject Alternative Name with attribute, name verification will be performed solely against Subject Alternative Name

- In the absence of Subject Alternative Name, or its attribute, name verification will be performed against Common Name

AnyConnect Client System Requirements

1. **Windows Requirements**

- Pentium class processor or greater

- 100 MB hard disk space

- Microsoft Installer, version 3.1

2. **Linux Requirements**

- x86 instruction set

- 64-bit processor

- 32 MB RAM

- 20 MB hard disk space

3. **Mac Requirements**

- AnyConnect requires 50MB of hard disk space

- To operate correctly with Mac, AnyConnect requires a minimum display resolution of 1024 by 640 pixels

Supported Operating Systems	Windows 7, 8, 8.1, 10, 10 RS1, RS2, & RS3 x86(32-bit) and x64(64-bit)	macOS 10.11, 10.12, and 10.13	Linux Red Hat 6, 7 & Ubuntu 14.04 (LTS) and 16.04 (LTS) (64-bit only)
VPN Client	Yes	Yes	Yes
Network Access Manager	Yes	No	No
Cloud Web Security	Yes	Yes	No
VPN Posture (HostScan)	Yes	Yes	Yes
ISE Posture	Yes	Yes	No
DART	Yes	Yes	Yes
Customer Experience Feedback	Yes	Yes	Yes
Network Visibility Module	Yes	Yes	Yes
AMP Enabler	Yes	Yes	No
Umbrella Roaming Security	Yes	Yes	No

Table 9- AnyConnect Client Supported Features and Modules

Remote Access VPN Consideration Based on Functional Requirements

This table can be consulted while deciding the right VPN solution as per requirement:

Use Case	Full Tunnelling SSL VPN	Clientless SSL VPN	Full Tunnelling IPsec VPN
Requirement of transparent Network with managed devices	Yes	No	Yes
Access from unmanaged devices via public internet	No	Yes	No
Requirement of controlled transparent access	Yes	No	Yes
Requirement of controlled access without installation of client	No	Yes	No

Table 10- Selecting Right Mode for VPN Deployment

The algorithm choices in SSL based Remote Access VPN Solution are:

Algorithm Role	Recommendations
User Authentication	Static/one time passwords or certificates
Server Authentication	RSA (certificates)
Protocol Versions	TLS 1.x, SSL 3.0
SSL/TLS based Session's Authentication and Integrity	SHA-1 HMAC
SSL/TLS based session's traffic encryption	RC4, AES-128 or 3DES

Table 11- SSL based Remote Access VPN Solution

IKE Remote Access VPN Extensions

IKE protocol has the following built-in features for IPSec remote access VPNs:

➤ *IKE Extended Authentication (XAUTH)*- XAUTH provides another layer of security after peers have been mutually authenticated each other by asking one-time username and password, which would be statically defined on VPN gateway

➤ *IKE Mode Configuration*- This feature allows VPN Gateway to configure number of network parameters on remote machine for example, tunnel interface IP addressing, DNS Server, WINS server and split tunnelling feature etc.

This table shows the algorithm choice in IPSec based Remote Access VPN Solution:

Algorithm Role	Recommendation
Peer Authentication	Pre-shared keys or certificates
IKE Session Encryption	AES-128 or 3DES
IKE Session Packet Authentication and Integrity	SHA-1 HMAC
Remote User Traffic Encryption	AES-128 or 3DES
Remote User Traffic Authentication and Integrity	SHA-1 HMAC
Key Exchange	Diffie-Hellman

Table 12- IPSec based Remote Access VPN Solution

Key lengths in above defined algorithms happen to be a critical part as far as effectiveness of certain algorithm is concerned. The following table shows the minimum key length recommendations for each of above defined algorithm:

Protection Period	Symmetric Method(3DES, AES,RC4) Minimum Key Length	Symmetric Method(HMAC) Minimum Key Length	Asymmetric Method(RSA and DH) Minimum Key Length
Short-term Protection (until 2012)	80	160	1248
Medium-term Protection (until 2020)	96	192	1776
Medium-term Protection (until 2030)	112	224	2432
Long-term Protection (until 2040)	128	256	3248

Table 13- Minimum Key Length Recommendations

High Availability Consideration for Remote Access VPN Solutions

Two of the most important factors that should be kept in mind while designing and installing certain networks are Redundancy and High Availability (HA). Remote users expect to have same kind of redundancy and uptime when working in corporate office.

In Remote Access (RA) VPN solutions, High Availability and Redundancy seldom go hand in hand due to inability to deploy RA VPN in active/active configuration. However, downtime or loss of service during failover can be reduced in number of ways including VPN clustering, Stateful failover and redundant peering.

The main HA and Redundancy methods being available in Cisco ASA devices are:

Hardware based Failover

The hardware-based failover is configurable between two Cisco ASA devices having same hardware configuration and software OS version. The two devices in failover configuration negotiate their current VPN sessions limits. For example, one of the failover

configured devices has AnyConnect premium licence for 250 users and another device has installed licence for 100 users, this means that overall failover pair supports up to 350 AnyConnect VPN sessions as long as this number does not exceed the current platform's limits. The only exception in this rule is for ASA 5505 and ASA 5510 devices, which requires Security Plus license to be installed first before failover configuration becomes available.

As far as software version of ASA is concerned, the major (first number), the minor (second number) and the maintenance (third number) software version running on both devices does not necessarily need to be same. For example, one can run 7.0(1) on one device and 7.0(4) on second device and still maintain the failover feature.

Two types of hardware based failover configuration are available namely, active/active and active/standby. Due to the creations of virtual contexts in active/active configuration, only active/standby failover configuration is applicable in scenarios where Remote Access VPN is deployed.

In active/standby configuration, one device remains active i.e. forwards as well as inspects the traffic, while the other device just monitors the status of active device. Once active device goes down, standby ASA starts performing. In addition to default functionality, active/standby configuration also supports following modes, which support the session continuation during a failover:

➢ **Stateful Mode**- Allows remote users sessions to remain open and working after a failover has occurred between two devices. Remote users remain unaware that failover has occurred and their regular work remains uninterrupted

➢ **Stateless Mode**- As the name depicts, this mode involves no synchronization of state tables between active and standby devices hence in the case of a failover, every connection and session get dropped and must be recreated again in order to start working again.

VPN Clustering (VPN Load Balancing)

VPN clustering provides redundancy to AnyConnect users by sharing and load balancing between devices in a cluster. One device is configured to act as a master and it will be responsible to handle the incoming connections and it will further distribute them to least loaded device in a cluster for further action. This method does not necessarily require each ASA device to have a same software version, however, a single device with no support for single configuration command can affect the whole cluster.

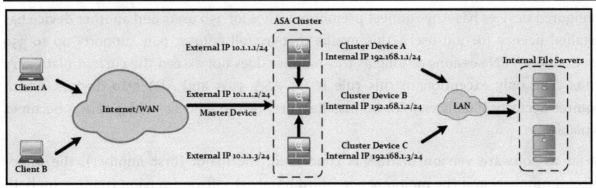

Figure 36- VPN Clustering

Redundant VPN Peering

IPsec as well as AnyConnect VPN client software allows multiple ASA addresses to be configured as VPN servers. In case primary ASA is failing and becoming unavailable, before client attempts to establish a new connection, VPN software tries to connect to next available address from the list of configured addresses. Similarly, client software can use the Dead Peer Detection (DPD) feature to detect the unavailability of ASA if connection between client and ASA has already been established. As this method of redundancy is totally client-side feature, so there is no formal requirement for software version of multiple ASA being configured as VPN peers in the client configuration.

External Load Balancing

Another option for implementing HA and redundancy is by using some external load balancing device for example, ACE 4710 appliance or a load balancer module in 6500/7600 series switch/router. The Application Control Engine (ACE) is configured with public IP address known as Virutal IP (VIP) that would be used in AnyConnect Connections as VPN peer address. Several ASAs can be configured behind ACE. Once a requests for VIP are received by ACE, it will load balance them between real ASAs behind it.

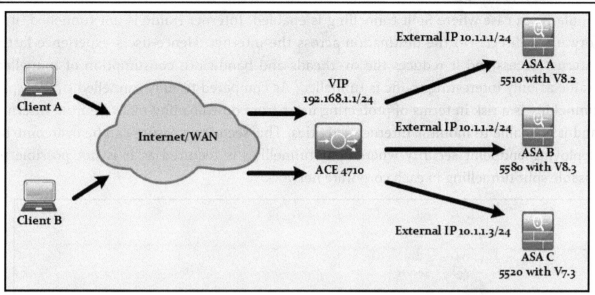

Figure 37- External Load Balancing Diagram

Split Tunnelling

While using a VPN, all traffic flowing across the network is using a secure encrypted tunnel. When Split tunnelling is not enabled in a VPN, VPN traffic generating from a corporate network is tunnelled to the remote private network across the internet. Similarly, the return traffic is tunnelled to reach another end. Internet traffic in this scenario first tunnelled to the remote network, then it goes to the internet destination. To understand this scenario, consider a company having remote clients connected to it with a Remote access VPN, where split tunnelling is disabled. All generated traffic no matter whether it is destined to the corporate network or internet, will be tunnelled to the remote private network. When split tunnelling is disabled, users face latency consumes bandwidth, however, in terms of security, when all traffic is tunnelled, all traffic can be inspected and monitored.

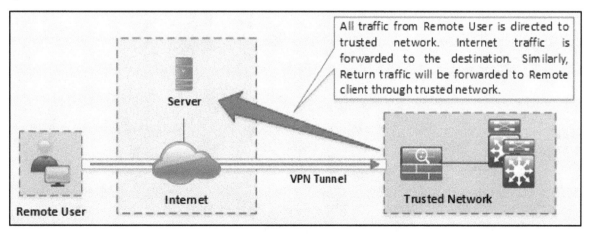

Figure 38- Split Tunnelling

73

Similarly, in case where Split tunnelling is enabled, Internet traffic is not tunnelled, it is forwarded directly to the destination across the internet. Hence users experience faster internet access and it reduces the overheads and bandwidth consumption of tunnelled traffic as only interesting traffic is tunnelled. As compared to fully tunnelled traffic, split tunnelling is a risk in terms of protecting users from downloading malware from internet and it is unable to monitor Internet activities. This security measure can be overcome by deploying endpoint security where split tunnelling is required as it is not possible to disable split tunnelling in each corporate network.

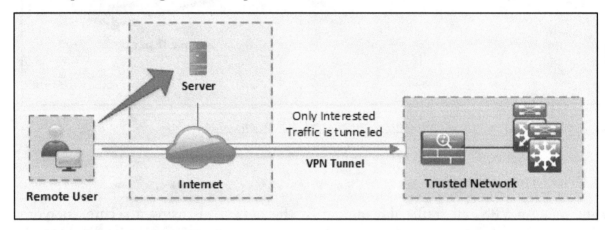

Figure 39- Split Tunnelling

Chapter 2: Secure Communications

Cisco AnyConnect Secure Mobility Client Installation

When installing AnyConnect client software for full tunnelling remote access VPN deployment, there are two options available to network administrator:

- Web deployment
- Manual deployment

Web Deployment Mode

Allows network administrator to push the AnyConnect client software towards the remote machine via URL address of VPN gateway. Remote Users, after browsing to the provided URL, can either download the software manually or will be prompted with the automatic download option. One of the major advantages of this option is automatic uninstallation of VPN client software after user has been disconnected. First, get the copy of AnyConnect software installation package (either in ZIP or PKG format) from Cisco.com website through a user's account with a valid support agreement.

The possible deployment packages depending on latest version of AnyConnect software and OS are:

Package	Platform
Anyconnect-win-version-k9.pkg	Microsoft Windows
Anyconnect-macOSX-i386-version-k9.pkg	Mac OS X
Anyconnect-linux-version-k9.pkg	Linux 32 bit
Anyconnect-linux-64-version-k9.pkg	Linux 64 bit

Table 14- Deployment Packages

After downloading the appropriate package, it needs to be uploaded in the flash of ASA by using HTTP/TFTP/FTP/SMB. To upload it via ASDM, click **Configuration** > **Remote Access VPN** > **Network (Client) Access** > **AnyConnect Client Software** and then click **Add**. After providing the local path to downloaded file, click **Upload**button.

After the upload gets completed, configuration of connection profile(s) is required to allow deployment of the AnyConnect client software. To do so, navigate to **Configuration** > **Remote Access VPN** > **Network (Client) Access** > **AnyConnect Client Profiles**. Secure Socket Layer (SSL) and AnyConnect Client access must be

enabled on relevant interfaces in order to complete the AnyConnect Web-based deployment. Enable DTLS option in case of latency or if delayed sensitive application requires VPN access.

Manual Deployment Mode

Remote users or support representatives may install VPN client software manually. If end machine is manageable for example, part of some internal domain etc., group policy can also be used to install the VPN client software automatically on end machines. One example in this regard is using Microsoft Group Policy feature.

Manual installation is pretty straightforward. First, get the copy of AnyConnect software installation package from Cisco.com web site through a user account with valid support agreement.

The possible pre-deployment files depending on latest version of AnyConnect software and OS are:

Filename	OS
Anyconnect-win-version-k9.iso	Microsoft Windows
Anyconnect-macOSX-i386-version-k9.dmg	Mac OS X DMG file
Anyconnect-linux_32-version-k9.tar.gz	Linux 32-bit TAR file
Anyconnect-Linux_64-version-k9.tar.gz	Linux 64-bit TAR file

Table 15- Pre-Deployment Packages

To keep things simple, as installation procedure in each OS varies, consider the installation procedure for windows based environment. After downloading the package, extract it.

This table contains the expected files within ISO file and its purpose:

File	Purpose
GUI.ico	AnyConnect icon image
Setup.exe	The installation utility
Anyconnect-dar-win-verion-k9.msi	Diagnostic and Reporting Tool (DART) optional module
Anyconnect-gina-version-predeploy-k9.msi	Start Before Login (SBL) optional module
Anyconnect-nam-win-version-k9.msi	Network Access Manager (NAM) optional module
Anyconnect-posture-win-version-predeploy-k9.msi	Posture optional module
Anyconnect-telemetry-win-version-predeploy-k9.msi	Telemetry optional module
Anyconnect-websecurity-win-version-predeploy-k9.msi	Web Security optional module
Anyconnect-win-version-predeploy-k9.msi	AnyConnect core client file
Autorun.inf	Auto run information file for Setup.exe
Cues_bg.jpg	A background image for the installation utility GUI
Setup.hta	Customizable Install Utility HTML Application (HTA)
Update.txt	A text file containing the AnyConnect version number
Eula_dialog.html Eula.html	File in HTML format containing the Cisco end user license agreement

Table 16- Expected Files within ISO File

To start the installation, run **setupe.exe** and this web page would appear:

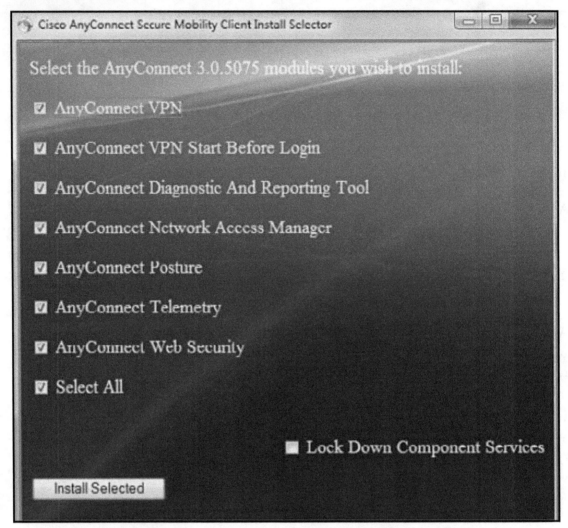

Figure 40- Cisco AnyConnect Secure Mobility Installation Page

The exact installation web page may depend on version of AnyConnect being used for installation. The diagram used in this workbook shows the installation procedure of AnyConnect version 3.0. From the menu being showed in above installation utility, optional modules can be installed along with AnyConnect core module. Without core module, the only optional modules that can be installed are Web Security, NAM and DART. The remaining modules require AnyConnect core client to be installed first.

The list of priority of installation is:

- AnyConnect Core Client software
- Web Security, Posture, SBL and NAM modules (in any order)
- Telemetry module (requires the installation of posture module first)

By selecting the Lock Down Component Services, selected modules will be installed without any user privileges. It means even administrator would not be allowed to stop or disable specific module. In order to revert the setting, the only available option is to reinstall the module.

The Setup.hta; an HTML file, contains the VBScript along with HTML code. This file can be edited with scripting languages to customize the options available in installation procedure to end users. For example, the following figure shows the customizable setup with few options and without Lock Down Component Services option:

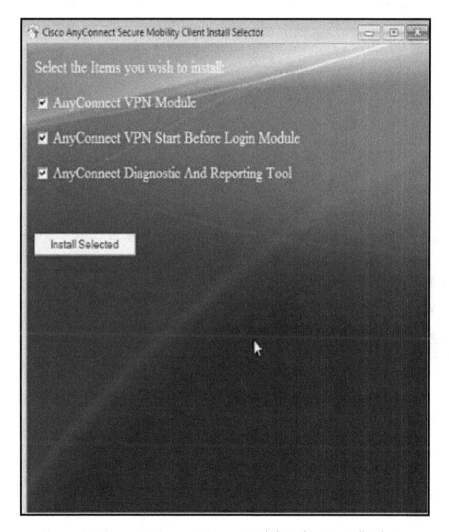

Figure 41- Cisco AnyConnect Secure Mobility Client Install Selector

Click the *Install Selected* button to start the installation of individual MSI files of selected modules. After installation of each module, a restart would be required to finally start using the AnyConnect VPN Client software.

The ultimate choice of deployment from above modes totally depends on the environment where full tunnelling remote access VPN solution is deployed. For example, if remote user spends most of time on the road, then web deployment based solution would be easier for end-user to access URL to the SSL VPN gateway then download and install the client software as per need.

While deploying AnyConnection based VPN connection, it is good to understand the environment prior to deployment. For example:

- Will the AnyConnect VPN be available to users being geographically disperse?
- Is there any possibility of users with multilingual background sharing the same working environment?
- What is the ratio of remote workers who are working constantly from corporate office as compared to the other remote working scenarios?

Answering these questions provide a great starting point in order to customize the AnyConnect client and overall deployment of full tunnelling VPN solution.

Lab 1.1: Implementing IPv4 IPSec with IKEv1

Case Study

Configure Site-to-Site IPSec Internet Key Exchange Version 1 (IKEv1) by using Command Line Interface in between Cisco Adaptive Security Appliance (ASA) and Cisco IOS router. Consider an organization implementing Site-to-Site VPN to connect the employees working in a branch office to its head office. Let us configure the Site-to-Site VPN using IKEv1.

Topology Diagram:

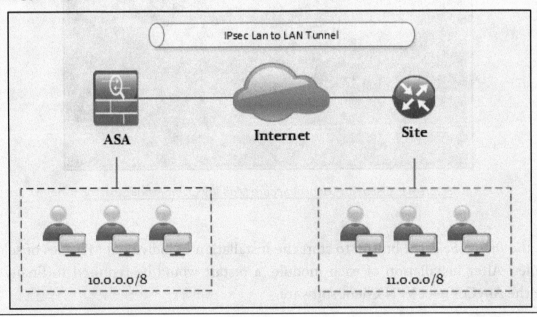

ASA Configuration:

ciscoasa(config)#hostname ASA

ASA(config)#enable password cisco

ASA(config)#passwd cisco

ASA(config)#interface Ethernet0

ASA(config-if)#nameif outside

ASA(config-if)#security-level 0

ASA(config-if)#ip address 172.16.1.1 255.255.255.0

ASA(config)#interface Ethernet1

ASA(config-if)#nameif inside

ASA(config-if)#security-level 100

ASA(config-if)#ip address 10.0.0.1 255.0.0.0

ASA(config)#access-list 100 extended permit ip 10.0.0.0 255.0.0.0 11.0.0.0 255.0.0.0

ASA(config)#access-list 101 extended permit ip 11.0.0.0 255.0.0.0 10.0.0.0 255.0.0.0

ASA(config)#access-list VPN-ACL extended permit ip 10.0.0.0 255.0.0.0 11.0.0.0 255.0.0.0

ASA(config)#access-group 101 in interface outside

ASA(config)#access-group 100 in interface inside

ASA(config)#router ospf 1

ASA(config-router)#network 10.0.0.0 255.0.0.0 area 0

ASA(config-router)#network 172.16.1.0 255.255.255.0 area 0

ASA(config)#crypto ikev1 policy 1

ASA(config-ikev1-policy)#authentication pre-share

ASA(config-ikev1-policy)#encryption des

ASA(config-ikev1-policy)#hash md5

ASA(config-ikev1-policy)#group 2

ASA(config-ikev1-policy)#lifetime 3600

ASA(config)#tunnel-group 1.0.0.2 type ipsec-l2l

ASA(config)#tunnel-group 1.0.0.2 ipsec-attributes

ASA(config-tunnel-ipsec)# ikev1 pre-shared-key IPS

ASA(config)#crypto ipsec ikev1 transform-set IPSEC esp-des esp-md5-hmac

ASA(config)#crypto map IPSEC-CRYPTOMAP 10 match address VPN-ACL

ASA(config)#crypto map IPSEC-CRYPTOMAP 10 set peer 1.0.0.2

ASA(config)#crypto map IPSEC-CRYPTOMAP 10 set ikev1 transform-set IPSEC

ASA(config)#crypto map IPSEC-CRYPTOMAP interface outside

ASA(config)#crypto ikev1 enable outside

Router Configuration:

Router(config)#hostname Site

Site(config)#crypto isakmp policy 1

Site(config-ikev1-policy)#hash md5

Site(config-ikev1-policy)#authentication pre-share

Site(config-ikev1-policy)#group 2

Site(config-ikev1-policy)#lifetime 3600

Site(config)#crypto isakmp key IPS address 172.16.1.1

Site(config)#crypto ipsec transform-set IPSEC esp-des esp-md5-hmac

Site(config)#crypto map IPSEC-CRYPTOMAP 1 ipsec-isakmp

Site(config-crypto-map)#set peer 172.16.1.1

```
Site(config-crypto-map)#set transform-set IPSEC
Site(config-crypto-map)#match address VPN-ACL


Site(config)#interface FastEtherneto/o
Site(config-if)#ip address 1.0.0.2 255.255.255.252
Site(config-if)#duplex auto
Site(config-if)#speed auto
Site(config-if)#crypto map IPSEC-CRYPTOMAP


Site(config)#interface FastEtherneto/1
Site(config-if)#ip address 11.0.0.1 255.0.0.0
Site(config-if)#duplex auto
Site(config-if)#speed auto


Site(config)#router ospf 1
Site(config-router)#network 1.0.0.0 0.0.0.3 area 0
Site(config-router)#network 11.0.0.0 0.255.255.255 area 0


Site(config)#ip access-list extended VPN-ACL
Site(config-ext-nacl)#permit ip 11.0.0.0 0.255.255.255 10.0.0.0 0.255.255.255
```

Verification:

Ping from Site LAN Network to the Remote LAN Network to check the Connectivity.

Ping 10.0.0.10

```
🖳 VPC3                                                        —  □  ✕

VPCS> ping 10.0.0.10

84 bytes from 10.0.0.10 icmp_seq=1 ttl=63 time=40.654 ms
84 bytes from 10.0.0.10 icmp_seq=2 ttl=63 time=28.674 ms
84 bytes from 10.0.0.10 icmp_seq=3 ttl=63 time=28.246 ms
84 bytes from 10.0.0.10 icmp_seq=4 ttl=63 time=27.834 ms
84 bytes from 10.0.0.10 icmp_seq=5 ttl=63 time=27.318 ms

VPCS> █
```

Issue the Command **Traceroute 10.0.0.10 source 11.0.0.1** from Site Router to check the route used for reaching the destination Host.

Traceroute 10.0.0.10 source 11.0.0.1

```
🖳 37255                                                       —  □  ✕
Site#
Site#traceroute 10.0.0.10 source 11.0.0.1

Type escape sequence to abort.
Tracing the route to 10.0.0.10

  1
*Mar  1 01:23:59.523: ISAKMP:(1002):purging node -181002086110.0.0.10 120 msec 9
2 msec 44 msec
Site#
Site#█
```

Lab 1.2: Implementing IPv4 IPSec with IKEv2

Case Study

Configure Site-to-Site IPSec Internet Key Exchange Version 2 (IKEv2) by using Command Line Interface in between Cisco IOS routers. Consider an organization implementing Site-to-Site VPN to connect the employees working in a branch office, running network 11.0.0.0/8 to its head office, running the network 10.0.0.0/8. Let us configure the Site-to-Site VPN using IKEv2.

Topology Diagram:

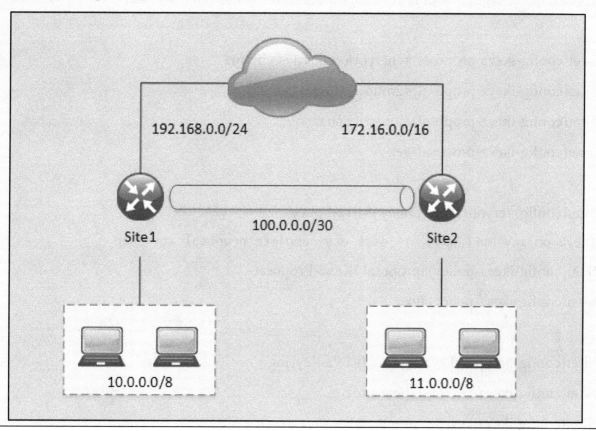

Site1 Configuration:

Note: Cloud and Router interfaces are pre-configured.

:

Site1(config)#int tunnel 0

Site1(config-if)#ip add 100.0.0.1 255.255.255.252

Site1(config-if)#tunnel source eth 0/1

Site1(config-if)#tunnel destination 172.16.0.1

Site1(config-if)#tunnel mode ipsec ipv4

Site1(config-if)#ex

Site1(config)#crypto ikev2 proposal IKEv2-Proposal

```
IKEv2 proposal MUST either have a set of an encryption algorithm other than
aes-gcm, an integrity algorithm and a DH group configured or encryption
algorithm aes-gcm, a prf algorithm and a DH group configured.
```

Site1(config-ikev2-proposal)#encryption des aes-cbc-192

Site1(config-ikev2-proposal)#group 2

Site1(config-ikev2-proposal)#integrity sha256

Site1(config-ikev2-proposal)#ex

Site1(config)#crypto ikev2 policy IKEv2-Policy

```
IKEv2 policy MUST have at least one complete proposal attached
```

Site1(config-ikev2-policy)#proposal IKEv2-Proposal

Site1(config-ikev2-policy)#ex

Site1(config)#crypto ikev2 keyring IKEv2-Keyring

Site1(config-ikev2-keyring)#peer site2

Site1(config-ikev2-keyring-peer)#address 172.16.0.1

Site1(config-ikev2-keyring-peer)#pre-shared-key ipspecialist

Site1(config-ikev2-keyring-peer)#ex

Site1(config)#crypto ikev2 profile IKEv2-Profile

```
IKEv2 profile MUST have:
    1. A local and a remote authentication method.
    2. A match identity or a match certificate or match any statement.
```

Site1(config-ikev2-profile)#identity local fqdn ipspecialist1.net

```
Site1(config-ikev2-profile)#match identity remote fqdn ipspecialist2.net

Site1(config-ikev2-profile)#authentication local pre-share

Site1(config-ikev2-profile)#authentication remote pre-share

Site1(config-ikev2-profile)#keyring local IKEv2-Keyring


Site1(config)#crypto ipsec transform-set IKEv2-TSET esp-3des esp-sha-hmac

Site1(config)#crypto ipsec profile IKEv2-Profile

Site1(ipsec-profile)#set transform-set IKEv2-TSET

Site1(ipsec-profile)#set ikev2-profile IKEv2-Profile

Site1(ipsec-profile)#ex

config t

Site1(config)#


Site1(config)#int tunnel 0

Site1(config-if)#tunnel protection ipsec profile IKEv2-Profile

Site1(config-if)#ex

Site1(config)#ip route 11.0.0.0 255.0.0.0 tunnel 0
```

Site2 Configuration:

```
Site2(config)#int eth 0/0

Site2(config-if)#ip add 11.0.0.1 255.0.0.0

Site2(config-if)#no sh

Site2(config-if)#ex


Site2(config)#int tunnel 0

Site2(config-if)#ip add 100.0.0.2 255.255.255.252

Site2(config-if)#no sh

Site2(config-if)#tunnel source eth 0/1
```

Site2(config-if)#tunnel destination 192.168.0.1

Site2(config-if)#tunnel mode ipsec ipv4

Site2(config-if)#ex

Site2(config)#crypto ikev2 proposal IKEv2-Proposal

```
IKEv2 proposal MUST either have a set of an encryption algorithm other than
aes-gcm, an integrity algorithm and a DH group configured or encryption
algorithm aes-gcm, a prf algorithm and a DH group configured.
```

Site2(config-ikev2-proposal)#encryption des aes-cbc-192

Site2(config-ikev2-proposal)#group 2

Site2(config-ikev2-proposal)#integrity sha256

Site2(config-ikev2-proposal)#ex

Site2(config)#crypto ikev2 policy IKEv2-Policy

```
IKEv2 policy MUST have at least one complete proposal attached.
```

Site2(config-ikev2-policy)#proposal IKEv2-Proposal

Site2(config-ikev2-policy)#ex

Site2(config)#crypto ikev2 keyring IKEv2-Keyring

Site2(config-ikev2-keyring)#peer site1

Site2(config-ikev2-keyring-peer)#address 192.168.0.1

Site2(config-ikev2-keyring-peer)#pre-shared-key ipspecialist

Site2(config-ikev2-keyring-peer)#ex

Site2(config-ikev2-keyring)#ex

Site2(config)#crypto ikev2 profile IKEv2-Profile

```
IKEv2 profile MUST have:
    1. A local and a remote authentication method.
    2. A match identity or a match certificate or match any statement.
```

Site2(config-ikev2-profile)#identity local fqdn ipspecialist2.net

Site2(config-ikev2-profile)#match identity remote fqdn ipspecialist1.net

Site2(config-ikev2-profile)#authentication local pre-share

Site2(config-ikev2-profile)#keyring local IKEv2-Keyring

Site2(config-ikev2-profile)#ex

Site2(config)#crypto ipsec transform-set IKEv2-TSET esp-3des esp-sha-hmac

Site2(cfg-crypto-trans)#ex

Site2(config)#crypto ipsec profile IKEv2-Profile

Site2(ipsec-profile)#set transform-set IKEv2-TSET

Site2(ipsec-profile)#set ikev2-profile IKEv2-Profile

Site2(ipsec-profile)#ex

Site2(config)#int tunnel 0

Site2(config-if)#tunnel protection ipsec profile IKEv2-Profile

Site2(config-if)#ex

Site2(config)#ip route 10.0.0.0 255.0.0.0 tunnel 0

Verification

Ping from LAN 10.0.0.0/8 to remote site in order to check Layer 3 Connectivity.

Ping 11.0.0.10

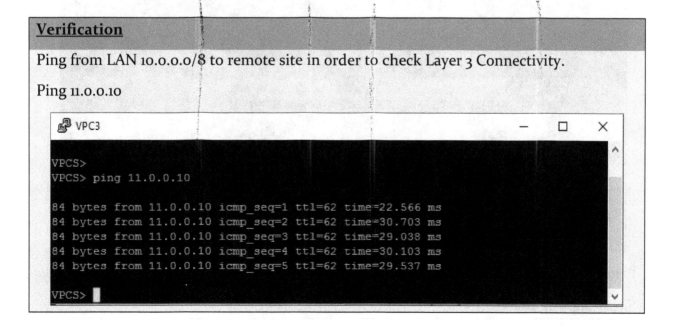

```
VPCS>
VPCS> ping 11.0.0.10

84 bytes from 11.0.0.10 icmp_seq=1 ttl=62 time=22.566 ms
84 bytes from 11.0.0.10 icmp_seq=2 ttl=62 time=30.703 ms
84 bytes from 11.0.0.10 icmp_seq=3 ttl=62 time=29.038 ms
84 bytes from 11.0.0.10 icmp_seq=4 ttl=62 time=30.103 ms
84 bytes from 11.0.0.10 icmp_seq=5 ttl=62 time=29.537 ms

VPCS>
```

Ping is successful!

Now, from Site1 Router, trace the path to the destination 11.0.0.0/8 network to verify if it is using Tunnel 0.

```
Site1                                               —  □  ✕

Site1#traceroute 11.0.0.10 source 10.0.0.1
Type escape sequence to abort.
Tracing the route to 11.0.0.10
VRF info: (vrf in name/id, vrf out name/id)
  1 100.0.0.2 40 msec 30 msec 30 msec
  2 11.0.0.10 31 msec 39 msec 31 msec
Site1#
Site1#
```

The output shows that tunnel 0 is being used for destination 11.0.0.0/8 network. 100.0.0.0/30 is the address assigned to the tunnel 0.

Site1# show ip route

```
Site1                                               —  □  ✕

Site1>en
Site1#show ip route
Codes: L - local, C - connected, S - static, R - RIP, M - mobile, B - BGP
       D - EIGRP, EX - EIGRP external, O - OSPF, IA - OSPF inter area
       N1 - OSPF NSSA external type 1, N2 - OSPF NSSA external type 2
       E1 - OSPF external type 1, E2 - OSPF external type 2
       i - IS-IS, su - IS-IS summary, L1 - IS-IS level-1, L2 - IS-IS level-2
       ia - IS-IS inter area, * - candidate default, U - per-user static route
       o - ODR, P - periodic downloaded static route, H - NHRP, l - LISP
       a - application route
       + - replicated route, % - next hop override

Gateway of last resort is not set

      1.0.0.0/30 is subnetted, 1 subnets
O        1.0.0.0 [110/20] via 192.168.0.2, 00:01:06, Ethernet0/1
      10.0.0.0/8 is variably subnetted, 2 subnets, 2 masks
C        10.0.0.0/8 is directly connected, Ethernet0/0
L        10.0.0.1/32 is directly connected, Ethernet0/0
S     11.0.0.0/8 is directly connected, Tunnel0
      100.0.0.0/8 is variably subnetted, 2 subnets, 2 masks
C        100.0.0.0/30 is directly connected, Tunnel0
L        100.0.0.1/32 is directly connected, Tunnel0
O     172.16.0.0/16 [110/30] via 192.168.0.2, 00:00:40, Ethernet0/1
      192.168.0.0/24 is variably subnetted, 2 subnets, 2 masks
C        192.168.0.0/24 is directly connected, Ethernet0/1
L        192.168.0.1/32 is directly connected, Ethernet0/1
Site1#
```

Output shows that 11.0.0.0/8 is connected via tunnel 0.

Site2# show ip route

```
Site2 _ □ ✕

Site2#show ip route
Codes: L - local, C - connected, S - static, R - RIP, M - mobile, B - BGP
       D - EIGRP, EX - EIGRP external, O - OSPF, IA - OSPF inter area
       N1 - OSPF NSSA external type 1, N2 - OSPF NSSA external type 2
       E1 - OSPF external type 1, E2 - OSPF external type 2
       i - IS-IS, su - IS-IS summary, L1 - IS-IS level-1, L2 - IS-IS level-2
       ia - IS-IS inter area, * - candidate default, U - per-user static route
       o - ODR, P - periodic downloaded static route, H - NHRP, l - LISP
       a - application route
       + - replicated route, % - next hop override

Gateway of last resort is not set

      1.0.0.0/30 is subnetted, 1 subnets
O        1.0.0.0 [110/20] via 172.16.0.2, 00:02:43, Ethernet0/1
O     10.0.0.0/8 [110/1010] via 100.0.0.1, 00:02:33, Tunnel0
      11.0.0.0/8 is variably subnetted, 2 subnets, 2 masks
C        11.0.0.0/8 is directly connected, Ethernet0/0
L        11.0.0.1/32 is directly connected, Ethernet0/0
      100.0.0.0/8 is variably subnetted, 2 subnets, 2 masks
C        100.0.0.0/30 is directly connected, Tunnel0
L        100.0.0.2/32 is directly connected, Tunnel0
      172.16.0.0/16 is variably subnetted, 2 subnets, 2 masks
C        172.16.0.0/16 is directly connected, Ethernet0/1
L        172.16.0.1/32 is directly connected, Ethernet0/1
O     192.168.0.0/24 [110/30] via 172.16.0.2, 00:02:43, Ethernet0/1
Site2#
```

Output shows that 10.0.0.0/8 is connected via tunnel 0.

Lab 1.3: Implementing DMVPN IPv4 Hub-Spoke and Spoke-Spoke

Case Study

Configure Site-to-Site IPv4 DMVPN by using Next Hop Redundancy Protocol (NHRP) and Border Gateway Protocol (BGP). Consider an organization implementing DMVPN to connect the Spoke (branch offices) to the Hub (head office). Let us configure the DMVPN Hub and Spokes.

Topology Diagram:

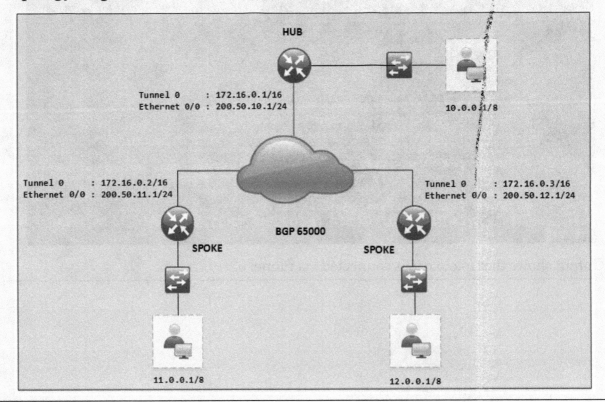

Hub (R1) Configuration:

R1>en

R1#config t

```
Enter configuration commands, one per line.  End with CNTL/Z.
```

R1(config)#int tunnel 0

```
*Aug  22  11:02:26.406:  %LINEPROTO-5-UPDOWN:  Line  protocol  on  Interface  Tunnel0,
changed state to down
```

R1(config-if)#ip add 172.16.0.1 255.255.255.0

R1(config-if)#ip nhrp map multicast dynamic

R1(config-if)#ip nhrp network-id 90

R1(config-if)#tunnel source eth 0/0

R1(config-if)#tunnel mode gre multipoint

```
*Aug 22 11:04:10.991: %LINEPROTO-5-UPDOWN: Line protocol on Interface Tunnel0,
changed state to up.
```

R1(config-if)#tunnel key 90

R1(config-if)#ip mtu 1400

R1(config-if)#ip tcp ad

R1(config-if)#ip tcp adjust-mss 1360

R1(config-if)#ex

R1(config)#router bgp 65000

R1(config-router)#bgp log-neighbor-changes

R1(config-router)#bgp listen range 172.16.0.0/24 peer-group DMVPN

R1(config-router)#neighbor DMVPN peer-group

R1(config-router)#neighbor DMVPN remote-as 65000

R1(config-router)#neighbor DMVPN route-reflector-client

R1(config-router)#neighbor DMVPN password P@$$word:10

R1(config-router)#network 10.0.0.0 mask 255.0.0.0

R1(config-router)#ex

Spoke 1 (R2) Configuration:

R2>

R2>en

R2#config t

```
Enter configuration commands, one per line.  End with CNTL/Z.
```

R2(config)#int tunnel 0

```
*Aug 22 11:08:29.252: %LINEPROTO-5-UPDOWN: Line protocol on Interface Tunnel0,
changed state to down
```

R2(config-if)#ip add 172.16.0.2 255.255.255.0

R2(config-if)#ip nhrp map multicast 200.50.10.1

R2(config-if)#ip nhrp map 172.16.0.1 200.50.10.1

R2(config-if)#ip nhrp nhs 172.16.0.1

R2(config-if)#ip nhrp network-id 90

R2(config-if)#tunnel source eth 0/0

R2(config-if)#tunnel destination 200.50.10.1

```
*Aug 22 11:10:15.522: %LINEPROTO-5-UPDOWN: Line protocol on Interface Tunnel0,
changed state to up
```

R2(config-if)#tunnel key 90

R2(config-if)#ex

R2(config)#router bgp 65000

R2(config-router)#bgp log

R2(config-router)#bgp log-neighbor-changes

R2(config-router)#network 11.0.0.0 mask 255.0.0.0

R2(config-router)#neighbor 172.16.0.1 remote-as 65000

R2(config-router)#neighbor 172.16.0.1 password P@$$word:10

R2(config-router)#ex

```
*Aug 22 11:12:14.413: %BGP-5-ADJCHANGE: neighbor 172.16.0.1 Up
```

Spoke 2 (R3) Configuration:

R3#config t

```
Enter configuration commands, one per line.  End with CNTL/Z.
```

R3(config)#int tunnel 0

```
*Aug 22 11:27:21.000: %LINEPROTO-5-UPDOWN: Line protocol on Interface Tunnel0,
changed state to down
```

R3(config-if)#ip add 172.16.0.3 255.255.255.0

R3(config-if)#ip nhrp map multicast 200.50.10.1

R3(config-if)#ip nhrp map 172.16.0.1 200.50.10.1

R3(config-if)#ip nhrp nhs 172.16.0.1

R3(config-if)#ip nhrp network-id 90

R3(config-if)#tunnel source eth 0/0

R3(config-if)#tunnel destination 200.50.10.1

```
*Aug 22 11:28:57.125: %LINEPROTO-5-UPDOWN: Line protocol on Interface Tunnel0,
changed state to up
```

R3(config-if)#tunnel key 90

R3(config-if)#ex

R3(config)#router bgp 65000

R3(config-router)#bgp log-neighbor-changes

R3(config-router)#network 12.0.0.0 mask 255.0.0.0

R3(config-router)#neighbor 172.16.0.1 remote-as 65000

R3(config-router)#neighbor 172.16.0.1 password P@$$word:10

```
*Aug 22 11:30:48.306: %BGP-5-ADJCHANGE: neighbor 172.16.0.1 Up
```

Verification:

Ping from 11.0.0.1 to 12.0.0.1 for connectivity verification.

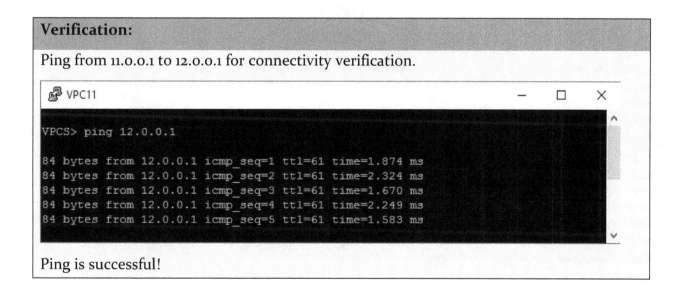

Ping is successful!

Lab 1.4: Implementing DMVPN IPv6 over IPv4

Case Study

Configure Site-to-Site IPv6 DMVPN by using Next Hop Redundancy Protocol (NHRP) and Border Gateway Protocol (BGP). Consider an organization implementing DMVPN to connect the Spoke (branch offices) to the Hub (head office). Let usp configure the DMVPN Hub and Spokes.

Topology Diagram:

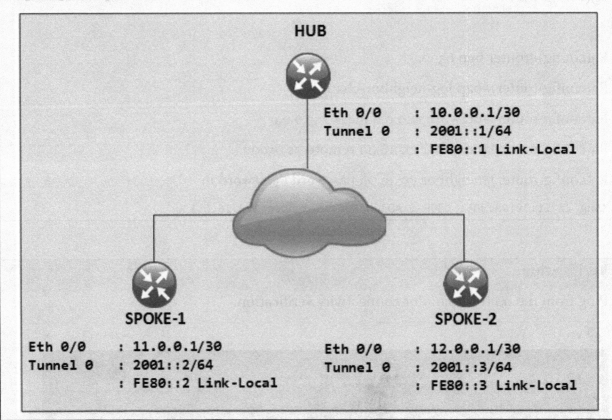

HUB:
Router(config)#hostname HUB
HUB(config)#ipv6 unicast-routing
HUB(config)#int eth 0/0
HUB(config-if)#ip add 10.0.0.1 255.255.255.252
HUB(config-if)#no sh
HUB(config-if)#ex
*Aug 23 06:33:11.277: %LINK-3-UPDOWN: Interface Ethernet0/0, changed state to up

```
*Aug 23 06:33:12.285: %LINEPROTO-5-UPDOWN: Line protocol on Interface Ethernet0/0,
changed state to up
```

HUB(config)#router ospf 1

HUB(config-router)#network 10.0.0.0 0.0.0.3 area 0

HUB(config-router)#ex

```
*Aug 23 06:33:37.802: %OSPF-5-ADJCHG: Process 1, Nbr 14.0.0.1 on Ethernet0/0 from
LOADING to FULL, Loading Done
```

HUB(config)#int tunnel 0

```
*Aug 23 06:33:49.793: %LINEPROTO-5-UPDOWN: Line protocol on Interface Tunnel0,
changed state to down
```

HUB(config-if)#tunnel source 10.0.0.1

HUB(config-if)#tunnel mode gre multipoint

```
*Aug 23 06:34:18.797: %LINEPROTO-5-UPDOWN: Line protocol on Interface Tunnel0,
changed state to up
```

HUB(config-if)#ipv6 nhrp network-id 100

HUB(config-if)#ipv6 address FE80::1 link-local

HUB(config-if)#ipv6 address 2001::1/64

HUB(config-if)#ipv6 nhrp redirect

HUB(config-if)#ex

SPOKE-1:

Router(config)#hostname SPOKE-1

SPOKE-1(config)#int eth 0/0

SPOKE-1(config-if)#ip add 11.0.0.1 255.255.255.252

SPOKE-1(config-if)#no sh

SPOKE-1(config-if)#ex

```
*Aug 23 06:36:21.197: %LINK-3-UPDOWN: Interface Ethernet0/0, changed state to up
*Aug 23 06:36:22.198: %LINEPROTO-5-UPDOWN: Line protocol on Interface Ethernet0/0,
changed state to up
```

SPOKE-1(config)#router ospf 1

SPOKE-1(config-router)#network 11.0.0.0 0.0.0.3 area 0

SPOKE-1(config-router)#ex

```
*Aug 23 06:36:44.559: %OSPF-5-ADJCHG: Process 1, Nbr 15.0.0.1 on Ethernet0/0 from
LOADING to FULL, Loading Done
```

SPOKE-1(config)#ipv6 unicast-routing

SPOKE-1(config)#int tunnel 0

```
*Aug 23 06:36:59.252: %LINEPROTO-5-UPDOWN: Line protocol on Interface Tunnel0,
changed state to down
```

SPOKE-1(config-if)#tunnel source 11.0.0.1

SPOKE-1(config-if)#tunnel mode gre multipoint

```
*Aug 23 06:37:18.260: %LINEPROTO-5-UPDOWN: Line protocol on Interface Tunnel0,
changed state to up
```

SPOKE-1(config-if)#ipv6 nhrp network-id 100

SPOKE-1(config-if)#ipv6 address FE80::2 link-local

SPOKE-1(config-if)#ipv6 address 2001::2/64

SPOKE-1(config-if)#ipv6 nhrp shortcut

SPOKE-1(config-if)#ipv6 nhrp nhs 2001::1 nbma 10.0.0.1

SPOKE-1(config-if)#ex

SPOKE-2:
Router(config)#hostname SPOKE-2
SPOKE-2(config)#int eth 0/0
SPOKE-2(config-if)#ip add 12.0.0.1 255.255.255.252
SPOKE-2(config-if)#no sh
SPOKE-2(config-if)#ex
``` *Aug 23 06:39:27.163: %LINK-3-UPDOWN: Interface Ethernet0/0, changed state to up ```
``` *Aug 23 06:39:28.167: %LINEPROTO-5-UPDOWN: Line protocol on Interface Ethernet0/0, changed state to up ```

SPOKE-2(config)#router ospf 1

SPOKE-2(config-router)#network 12.0.0.0 0.0.0.3 area 0

SPOKE-2(config-router)#ex

```
*Aug 23 06:39:45.026: %OSPF-5-ADJCHG: Process 1, Nbr 15.0.0.2 on Ethernet0/0 from
LOADING to FULL, Loading Done
```

SPOKE-2(config)#ipv6 unicast-routing

SPOKE-2(config)#int tunnel 0

```
*Aug 23 06:39:57.025: %LINEPROTO-5-UPDOWN: Line protocol on Interface Tunnel0,
changed state to down
```

SPOKE-2(config-if)#tunnel source 12.0.0.1

SPOKE-2(config-if)#tunnel mode gre multipoint

```
*Aug 23 06:40:26.034: %LINEPROTO-5-UPDOWN: Line protocol on Interface Tunnel0,
changed state to up
```

SPOKE-2(config-if)#ipv6 nhrp network-id 100

SPOKE-2(config-if)#ipv6 address FE80::3 link-local

SPOKE-2(config-if)#ipv6 address 2001::3/64

SPOKE-2(config-if)#ipv6 nhrp shortcut

SPOKE-2(config-if)#ipv6 nhrp nhs 2001::1 nbma 10.0.0.1

SPOKE-2(config-if)#ex

Verification and Troubleshooting of DMVPN:

HUB# show ip interface brief

```
HUB#show ip int brief
Interface              IP-Address      OK? Method Status                 Protocol
Ethernet0/0            10.0.0.1        YES manual up                     up
Ethernet0/1            unassigned      YES unset  administratively down down
Ethernet0/2            unassigned      YES unset  administratively down down
Ethernet0/3            unassigned      YES unset  administratively down down
Tunnel0                unassigned      YES unset  up                     up
HUB#
HUB#
```

Ethernet Interface is up, and Tunnel Interface is up. Tunnel o does not have any IPv4 address.

HUB# show ipv6 interface brief

```
HUB#show ipv6 int brief
Ethernet0/0              [up/up]
    unassigned
Ethernet0/1              [administratively down/down]
    unassigned
Ethernet0/2              [administratively down/down]
    unassigned
Ethernet0/3              [administratively down/down]
    unassigned
Tunnel0                  [up/up]
    FE80::1
    2001::1
HUB#
```

Tunnel o having IPv6 addresses.

HUB# Show dmvpn

```
HUB#show dmvpn
Legend: Attrb --> S - Static, D - Dynamic, I - Incomplete
        N - NATed, L - Local, X - No Socket
        # Ent --> Number of NHRP entries with same NBMA peer
        NHS Status: E --> Expecting Replies, R --> Responding, W --> Waiting
        UpDn Time --> Up or Down Time for a Tunnel
==================================================================

Interface: Tunnel0, IPv6 NHRP Details
Type:Hub, Total NBMA Peers (v4/v6): 2
    1.Peer NBMA Address: 11.0.0.1
        Tunnel IPv6 Address: 2001::2
        IPv6 Target Network: 2001::2/128
        # Ent: 1, Status: UP, UpDn Time: 00:05:48, Cache Attrib: D
    2.Peer NBMA Address: 12.0.0.1
        Tunnel IPv6 Address: 2001::3
        IPv6 Target Network: 2001::3/128
        # Ent: 1, Status: UP, UpDn Time: 00:01:58, Cache Attrib: D

HUB#
HUB#
```

Hub having Information of both route, towards SPOKE-1 (11.0.0.1) and SPOKE-2 (12.0.0.1).

HUB# show ipv6 nhrp

```
🖳 HUB                                                    —    ☐    ✕

HUB#show ipv6 nhrp                                              ^
2001::2/128 via 2001::2
    Tunnel0 created 00:06:45, expire 01:53:14
    Type: dynamic, Flags: unique registered used nhop
    NBMA address: 11.0.0.1
2001::3/128 via 2001::3
    Tunnel0 created 00:02:55, expire 01:57:04
    Type: dynamic, Flags: unique registered used nhop
    NBMA address: 12.0.0.1
FE80::2/128 via 2001::2
    Tunnel0 created 00:06:45, expire 01:53:14
    Type: dynamic, Flags: unique registered
    NBMA address: 11.0.0.1
FE80::3/128 via 2001::3
    Tunnel0 created 00:02:55, expire 01:57:04
    Type: dynamic, Flags: unique registered
    NBMA address: 12.0.0.1
HUB#
HUB#
HUB#                                                           v
```

NHRP details with both addresses (IPv6 address and Link-Local address) of each Spoke on Hub.

SPOKE-2# **show dmvpn**

```
🖳 SPOKE-2                                                —    ☐    ✕

SPOKE-2#show dmvpn                                              ^
Legend: Attrb --> S - Static, D - Dynamic, I - Incomplete
        N - NATed, L - Local, X - No Socket
        # Ent --> Number of NHRP entries with same NBMA peer
        NHS Status: E --> Expecting Replies, R --> Responding, W --> Waiting
        UpDn Time --> Up or Down Time for a Tunnel
==================================================================

Interface: Tunnel0, IPv6 NHRP Details
Type:Spoke, Total NBMA Peers (v4/v6): 1
    1.Peer NBMA Address: 10.0.0.1
        Tunnel IPv6 Address: 2001::1
        IPv6 Target Network: 2001::1/128
        # Ent: 1, Status: UP, UpDn Time: 00:04:09, Cache Attrib: S

SPOKE-2#                                                        v
```

Spoke-2 initially has peering with Hub only.

SPOKE-2# show ipv6 nhrp

```
SPOKE-2                                               —    □    ✕

SPOKE-2#show ipv6 nhrp
2001::1/128 via 2001::1
    Tunnel0 created 00:04:49, never expire
    Type: static, Flags: used
    NBMA address: 10.0.0.1
FE80::1/128 via FE80::1
    Tunnel0 created 00:04:49, never expire
    Type: static, Flags: nhs-ll
    NBMA address: 10.0.0.1
SPOKE-2#
```

Initially, SPOKE-2 has only the information of Hub.

Testing connectivity from SPOKE-2 to Hhub.

SPOKE-2# **trace 2001::1**

```
SPOKE-2                                               —    □    ✕
SPOKE-2#trace 2001::1
Type escape sequence to abort.
Tracing the route to 2001::1

  1 2001::1 1 msec 1 msec 1 msec
SPOKE-2#
```

Testing connectivity from SPOKE-2 to SPOKE-1.

SPOKE-2# **trace 2001::2**

```
SPOKE-2                                               —    □    ✕
SPOKE-2#trace 2001::2
Type escape sequence to abort.
Tracing the route to 2001::2

  1 2001::1 1 msec
    2001::2 1 msec 0 msec
```

For the first time, Connected via 2001::1 (HUB). Now, SPOKE-2 will learn the Address and for the next time, it will connect directly to the SPOKE-1 dynamically.

```
SPOKE-2                                               —    □    ✕
SPOKE-2#ping 2001::2
Type escape sequence to abort.
Sending 5, 100-byte ICMP Echos to 2001::2, timeout is 2 seconds:
!!!!!
Success rate is 100 percent (5/5), round-trip min/avg/max = 1/1/1 ms
SPOKE-2#trace 2001::2
Type escape sequence to abort.
Tracing the route to 2001::2

  1 2001::2 1 msec 0 msec 0 msec
SPOKE-2#
```

Now, SPOKE-2 is directly connected with SPOKE-1.

```
SPOKE-2                                                    —    □    ✕

SPOKE-2#show dmvpn
Legend: Attrb --> S - Static, D - Dynamic, I - Incomplete
        N - NATed, L - Local, X - No Socket
        # Ent --> Number of NHRP entries with same NBMA peer
        NHS Status: E --> Expecting Replies, R --> Responding, W --> Waiting
        UpDn Time --> Up or Down Time for a Tunnel
========================================================================

Interface: Tunnel0, IPv6 NHRP Details
Type:Spoke, Total NBMA Peers (v4/v6): 2
    1.Peer NBMA Address: 10.0.0.1
        Tunnel IPv6 Address: 2001::1
        IPv6 Target Network: 2001::1/128
        # Ent: 1, Status: UP, UpDn Time: 00:39:19, Cache Attrib: S
    2.Peer NBMA Address: 11.0.0.1
        Tunnel IPv6 Address: 2001::2
        IPv6 Target Network: 2001::2/128
        # Ent: 1, Status: UP, UpDn Time: 00:31:03, Cache Attrib: D

SPOKE-2#
```

Compare this output to the output shown above. Now, SPOKE-2 has learned the Peer NBMA to the Address 11.0.0.1 with the **Dynamic** Attribute mentioned with "**D**" in the output from Hub.

Lab 1.5: Implementing Site-to-Site Flex VPN

Case Study

In this lab, we are going to Implement Site-to-Site Flex VPN using Cisco Routers. Consider a scenario of two Sites, Site-1 & Site-2 located apart from each other on a wide geographical area. The requirement is to provide connectivity among these sites using Flex VPN.

Topology Diagram:

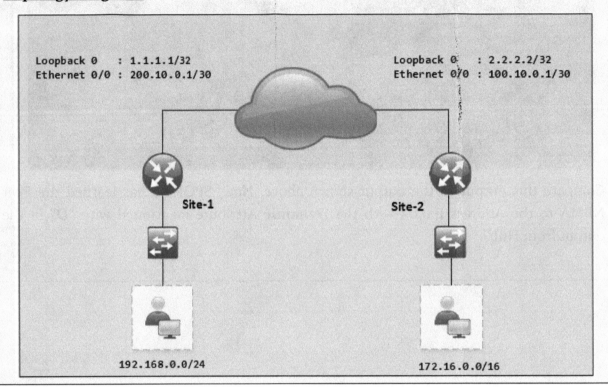

Site-1 Configuration:

R1(config)#ip domain-name ipspecialist.net

R1(config)#crypto ikev2 proposal IKEPROPOSAL

```
IKEv2 proposal MUST either have a set of an encryption algorithm other than aes-gcm,
an integrity algorithm and a DH group configured or encryption algorithm aes-gcm, a
prf algorithm and a DH group configured.
```

R1(config-ikev2-proposal)#encryption aes-cbc-256

R1(config-ikev2-proposal)#integrity sha512

R1(config-ikev2-proposal)#group 14

R1(config)#crypto ikev2 policy IKEPOLICY

```
IKEv2 policy MUST have at least one complete proposal attached.
```

R1(config-ikev2-policy)#match address local 200.10.0.1

R1(config-ikev2-policy)#proposal IKEPROPOSAL

R1(config)#crypto ikev2 keyring KEYRING

R1(config-ikev2-keyring)#peer R2

R1(config-ikev2-keyring-peer)#address 100.10.0.1

R1(config-ikev2-keyring-peer)#identity fqdn R2.ipspecialist.net

R1(config-ikev2-keyring-peer)#pre-shared-key local R1keyvpn

R1(config-ikev2-keyring-peer)#pre-shared-key remote R2keyvpn

R1(config-ikev2-keyring-peer)#ex

R1(config-ikev2-keyring)#ex

R1(config)#crypto ikev2 profile IKEPROFILE

```
IKEv2 profile MUST have:
    1. A local and a remote authentication method.
    2. A match identity or a match certificate or match any statement.
```

R1(config-ikev2-profile)#match identity remote fqdn R2.ipspecialist.net

R1(config-ikev2-profile)#identity local email R1@ipspecialist.net

R1(config-ikev2-profile)#authentication remote pre-share

R1(config-ikev2-profile)#authentication local pre-share

R1(config-ikev2-profile)#keyring local KEYRING

R1(config-ikev2-profile)#ex

R1(config)#crypto ipsec transform-set TSET esp-aes 256 esp-sha512-hmac

R1(cfg-crypto-trans)#mode tunnel

R1(cfg-crypto-trans)#ex

```
R1(config)#crypto ipsec profile IPSECPROFILE

R1(ipsec-profile)#set transform-set TSET

R1(ipsec-profile)#set ikev2-profile IKEPROFILE

R1(ipsec-profile)#ex


R1(config)#int tunnel 0

R1(config-if)#

*Aug 24 12:20:58.364: %LINEPROTO-5-UPDOWN: Line protocol on Interface Tunnel0,
changed state to down

R1(config-if)#tunnel source eth 0/0

R1(config-if)#ip unnumbered loopback0

R1(config-if)#

*Aug 24 12:21:26.081: %LINEPROTO-5-UPDOWN: Line protocol on Interface Loopback0,
changed state to up

R1(config-if)#tunnel mode ipsec ipv4

R1(config-if)#tunnel destination 100.10.0.1

R1(config-if)#tunnel path-mtu-discovery

R1(config-if)#tunnel protection ipsec profile IPSECPROFILE

R1(config-if)#

*Aug 24 12:22:16.831: %CRYPTO-6-ISAKMP_ON_OFF: ISAKMP is ON

R1(config-if)#ex


R1(config)#int loo

R1(config-if)#ip add 1.1.1.1 255.255.255.255

R1(config-if)#ex


R1(config)#router eigrp 100

R1(config-router)#network 1.1.1.1 0.0.0.0

R1(config-router)#network 192.168.0.0 0.0.0.255

R1(config-router)#ex
```

R1(config)#

Site-2 Configuration:

R1(config)# ip domain-name ipspecialist.net

R2(config)# crypto ikev2 proposal IKEPROPOSAL

```
IKEv2 proposal MUST either have a set of an encryption algorithm other than aes-gcm,
an integrity algorithm and a DH group configured or encryption algorithm aes-gcm, a
prf algorithm and a DH group configured.
```

R2(config-ikev2-proposal)# encryption aes-cbc-256

R2(config-ikev2-proposal)# integrity sha512

R2(config-ikev2-proposal)# group 14

R2(config)# crypto ikev2 policy IKEPOLICY

```
IKEv2 policy MUST have at least one complete proposal attached.
```

R2(config-ikev2-policy)# match address local 100.10.0.1

R2(config-ikev2-policy)# proposal IKEPROPOSAL

R2(config)#crypto ikev2 keyring KEYRING

R2(config-ikev2-keyring)# peer R1

R2(config-ikev2-keyring)# address 100.10.0.1

R2(config-ikev2-keyring)# identity email R1@ipspecialist.net

R2(config-ikev2-keyring)# pre-shared-key local R2keyvpn

R2(config-ikev2-keyring)# pre-shared-key remote R1keyvpn

R2(config)# crypto ikev2 profile IKEPROFILE

```
IKEv2 profile MUST have:
    1. A local and a remote authentication method.
    2. A match identity or a match certificate or match any statement.
```

R2(config-ikev2-profile)# match identity remote email R1@ipspecialist.net

R2(config-ikev2-profile)# identity local fqdn R2.ipspecialist.net

R2(config-ikev2-profile)# authentication remote pre-share

R2(config-ikev2-profile)# authentication local pre-share

R2(config-ikev2-profile)# keyring local KEYRING

R2(config)# crypto ipsec transform-set TSET esp-aes 256 esp-sha512-hmac

R2(cfg-crypto-trans)# mode tunnel

R2(config)#crypto ipsec profile IPSECPROFILE

R2(ipsec-profile)# set transform-set TSET

R2(ipsec-profile)# set ikev2-profile IKEPROFILE

R2(config)#interface Tunnel0

```
*Aug 24 13:28:58.364: %LINEPROTO-5-UPDOWN: Line protocol on Interface Tunnel0,
changed state to down
```

R1(config-if)#tunnel source eth 0/0

R2(config-if)# ip unnumbered Loopback0

```
*Aug 24 13:11:26.081: %LINEPROTO-5-UPDOWN: Line protocol on Interface Loopback0,
changed state to up
```

R2(config-if)# tunnel source Ethernet0/2

R2(config-if)# tunnel mode ipsec ipv4

R2(config-if)# tunnel destination 10.0.0.1

R2(config-if)# tunnel path-mtu-discovery

R2(config-if)# tunnel protection ipsec profile IPSECPROFILE

```
*Aug 24 12:22:16.831: %CRYPTO-6-ISAKMP_ON_OFF: ISAKMP is ON
```

R2(config)#router eigrp 10

R2(config-router)# network 2.2.2.2 0.0.0.0

R2(config-router)# network 172.16.0.254 0.0.0.0

Verification:

R1# **show ip route**

```
R1#show ip route
Codes: L - local, C - connected, S - static, R - RIP, M - mobile, B - BGP
       D - EIGRP, EX - EIGRP external, O - OSPF, IA - OSPF inter area
       N1 - OSPF NSSA external type 1, N2 - OSPF NSSA external type 2
       E1 - OSPF external type 1, E2 - OSPF external type 2
       i - IS-IS, su - IS-IS summary, L1 - IS-IS level-1, L2 - IS-IS level-2
       ia - IS-IS inter area, * - candidate default, U - per-user static route
       o - ODR, P - periodic downloaded static route, H - NHRP, l - LISP
       a - application route
       + - replicated route, % - next hop override

Gateway of last resort is not set

      1.0.0.0/8 is variably subnetted, 7 subnets, 2 masks
O        1.1.1.0/30 [110/20] via 200.10.0.2, 01:09:25, Ethernet0/0
C        1.1.1.1/32 is directly connected, Loopback0
O        1.1.1.4/30 [110/20] via 200.10.0.2, 01:09:12, Ethernet0/0
O        1.1.1.8/30 [110/20] via 200.10.0.2, 01:08:55, Ethernet0/0
O        1.1.1.12/30 [110/30] via 200.10.0.2, 00:56:43, Ethernet0/0
O        1.1.1.16/30 [110/30] via 200.10.0.2, 01:03:25, Ethernet0/0
O        1.1.1.20/30 [110/30] via 200.10.0.2, 01:03:25, Ethernet0/0
      2.0.0.0/32 is subnetted, 1 subnets
D        2.2.2.2 [90/27008000] via 2.2.2.2, 00:34:08, Tunnel0
      100.0.0.0/30 is subnetted, 1 subnets
O        100.10.0.0 [110/30] via 200.10.0.2, 00:57:14, Ethernet0/0
D     172.16.0.0/16 [90/26905600] via 2.2.2.2, 00:33:59, Tunnel0
      192.168.0.0/24 is variably subnetted, 2 subnets, 2 masks
C        192.168.0.0/24 is directly connected, Ethernet0/1
L        192.168.0.254/32 is directly connected, Ethernet0/1
      200.10.0.0/24 is variably subnetted, 2 subnets, 2 masks
C        200.10.0.0/30 is directly connected, Ethernet0/0
L        200.10.0.1/32 is directly connected, Ethernet0/0
R1#
```

As shown in the output,

```
      2.0.0.0/32 is subnetted, 1 subnets
D        2.2.2.2 [90/27008000] via 2.2.2.2, 00:34:08, Tunnel0
D     172.16.0.0/16 [90/26905600] via 2.2.2.2, 00:33:59, Tunnel0
```

These routes are learned by VPN Tunnel via EIGRP.

R1# **show ip int brief**

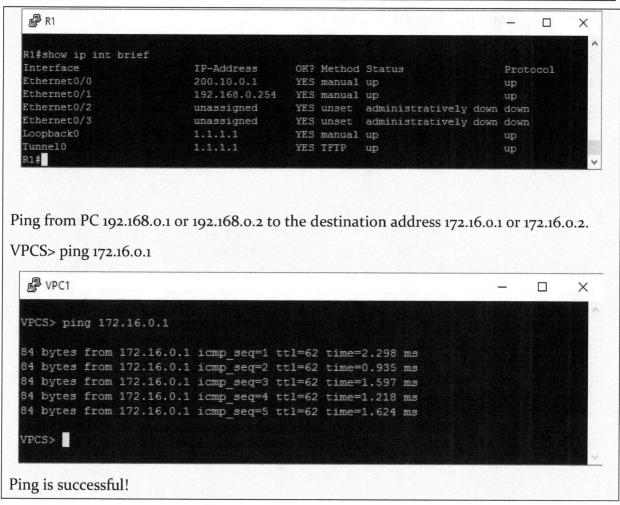

Ping from PC 192.168.0.1 or 192.168.0.2 to the destination address 172.16.0.1 or 172.16.0.2.

VPCS> ping 172.16.0.1

Ping is successful!

Lab 1.6 : Implementing Clientless SSL VPN on ASA

Case Study

In this lab, we are going to Implement Clientless SSL VPN on ASA

Topology Diagram:

SSL Clientless VPN Configuration

Access the firewall FW1 via Main Campus' Management station via ASDM.

Click [icon] inned to the task bar of management station, use the following credentials for login:

Username: IPSpecialist

Password: P@$$word:10

After successful login, the following dashboard should appear:

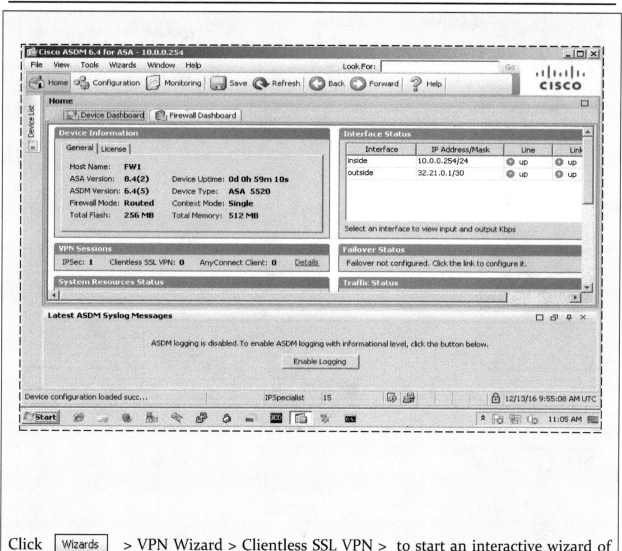

Click [Wizards] > VPN Wizard > Clientless SSL VPN > to start an interactive wizard of implementing the above SSL AnyConnect VPN.

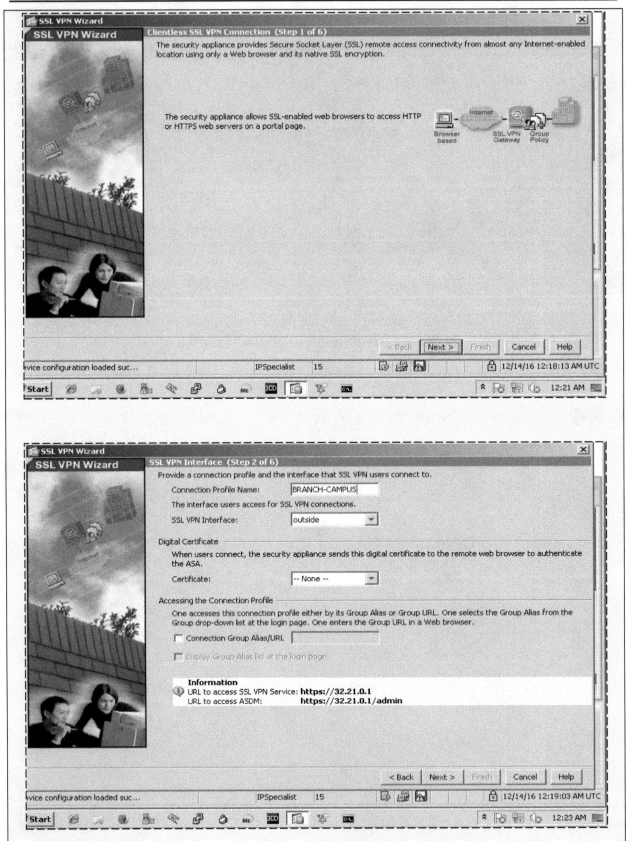

As shown in above figure, name the connection and click "Next".

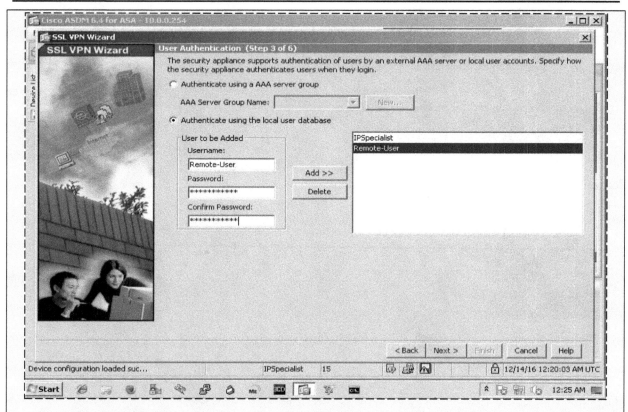

In the diagram above, local database on ASA will be used for authenticating users who want to connect via VPN. Other options include integration with ACS etc. Define the ! username with following credentials.

Username: Remote-User

Password: P@$$word:1o

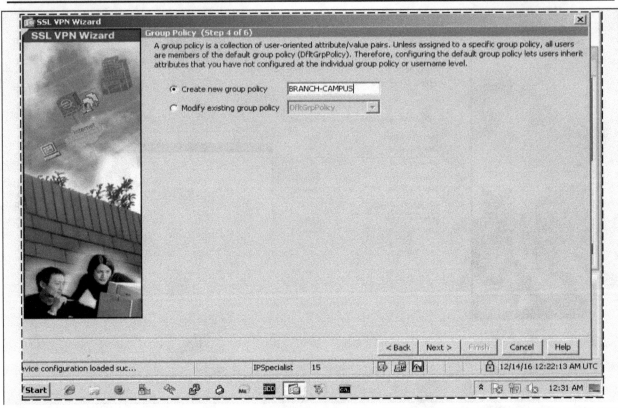

By clicking on "Manage" button, custom web URLs can be added, which can be accessed by users after connecting via clientless SSL VPN.

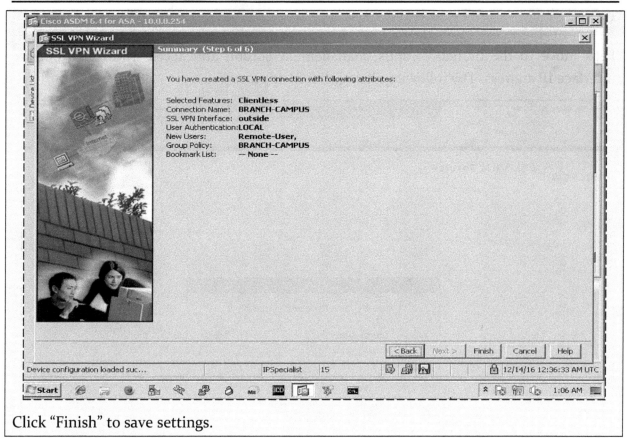

Click "Finish" to save settings.

ASA CLi Configuration:
Access the ASA via CLI and issue the following commands:
FW1(config)# webvpn
FW1 (config-webvpn)# no anyconnect-essentials
// Enable password for ASA is P@$$word:10

Verification:

Let's move to the branch campus' management station and access the ASA's outside interface IP address. The following dialog should appear.

Use the following credentials to successfully login via SSL Clientless VPN.

Username: Remote-User

Password: P@$$word:10

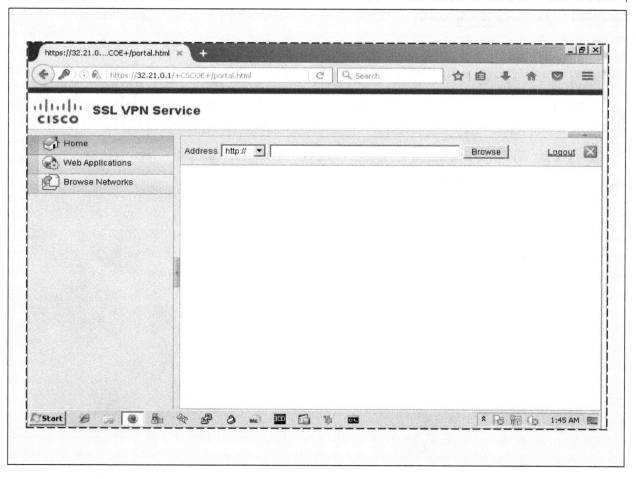

In order to check the active VPN connections via ASDM, click Monitoring > VPN > VPN Statistics > Sessions.

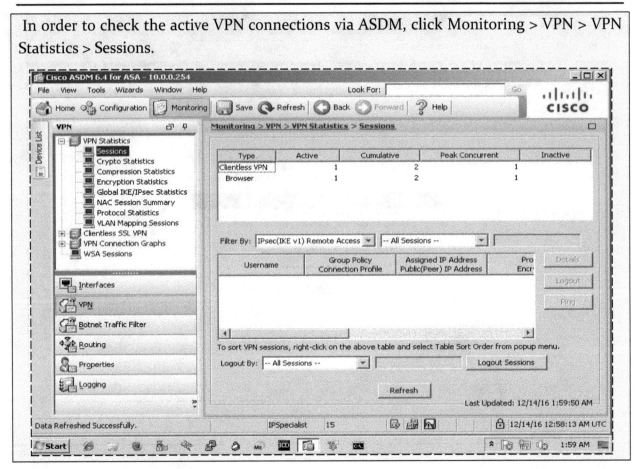

Implementing AnyConnet SSL VPN on ASA

Implement SSL AnyConnect VPN using CLI and ASDM for accessing Main Campus from Branch Campus.

In this lab, the main objective is to access the Main campus network securely via AnyConnect SSL VPN, which provides web browser based secure access.

The following topology will be used in this lab:

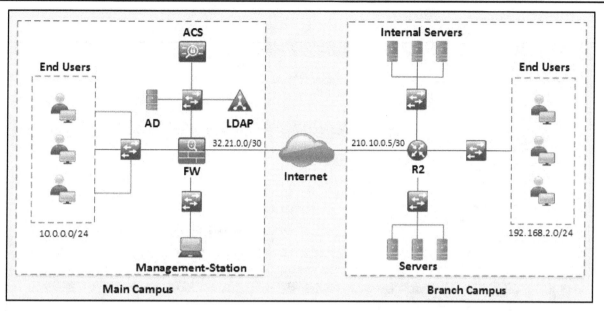

SSL AnyConnect VPN Configuration

Access the firewall FW1 via Main Campus' Management station via ASDM.

Open Cisco ASDM-IDM Launcher application, use the following credentials for login:

Username: IPSpecialist

Password: P@$$word:10

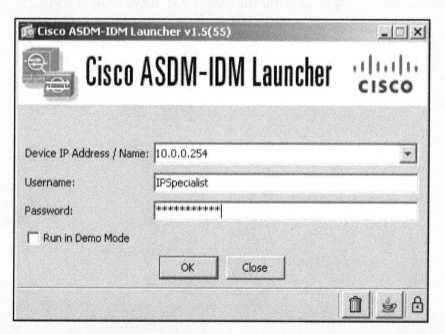

After successful login, the following dashboard should appear:

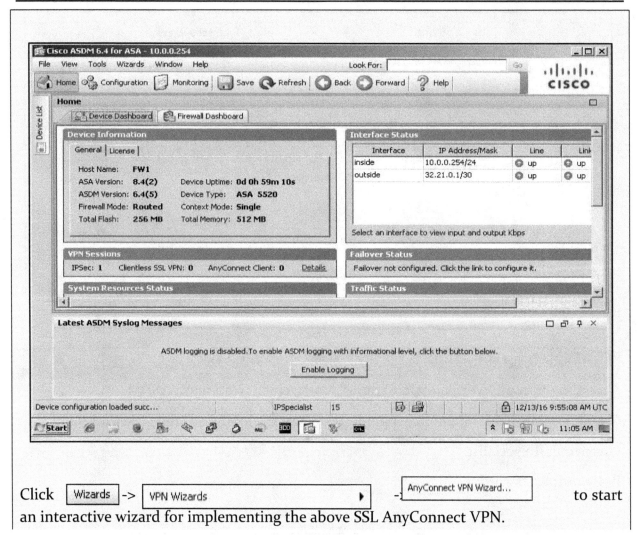

Click [Wizards] -> [VPN Wizards ▶] -[AnyConnect VPN Wizard...] to start an interactive wizard for implementing the above SSL AnyConnect VPN.

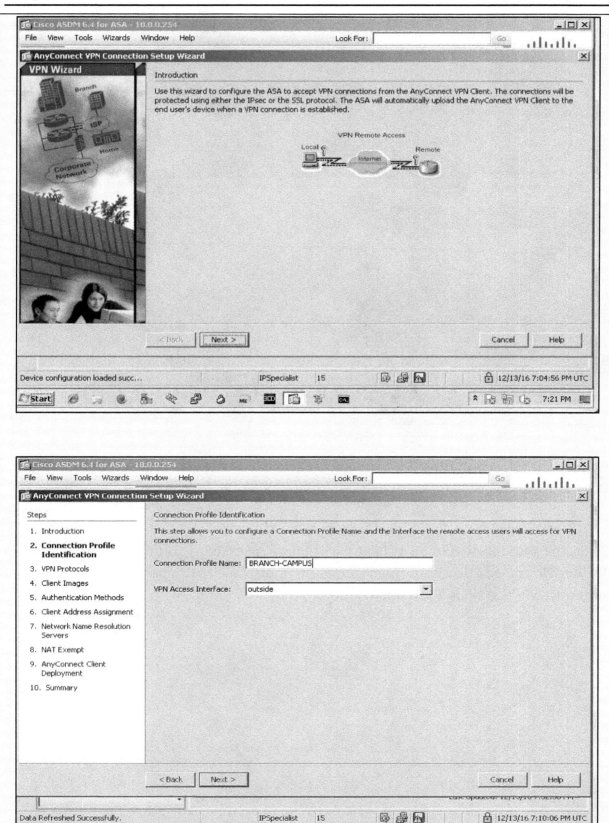

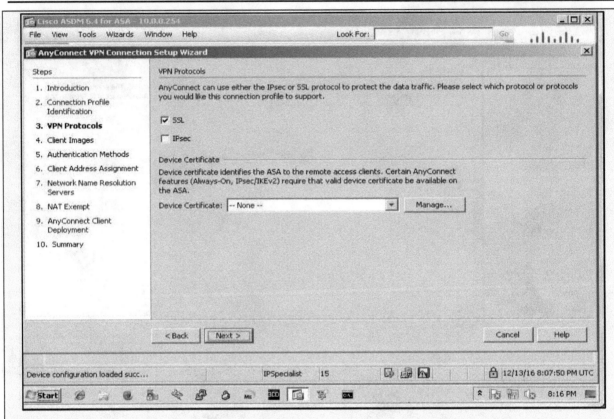

Select only SSL option IPsec Anyconnect VPN, which was implemented in last section. Click "Next".

Next, the path for AnyConnect client package will be asked. This information is available in the "Downloads" folder of "Management Station". Select the package for windows as client used in this lab is Microsoft Windows 7 based.

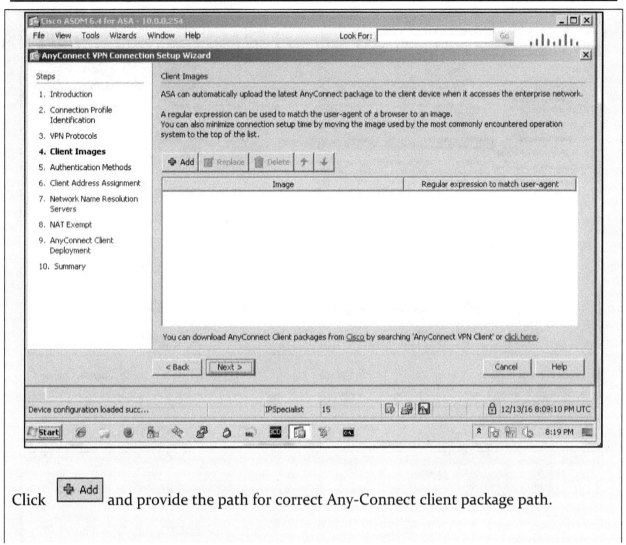

Click and provide the path for correct Any-Connect client package path.

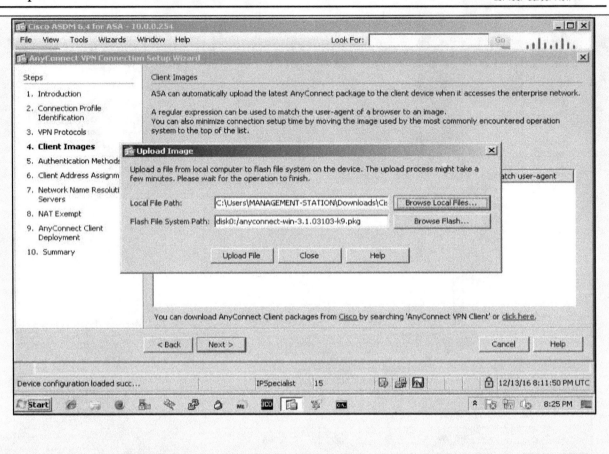

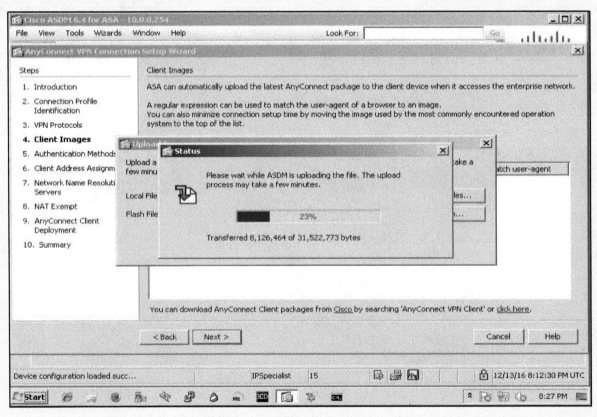

After successfully uploading the file, click "Next". The following dialog will appear.

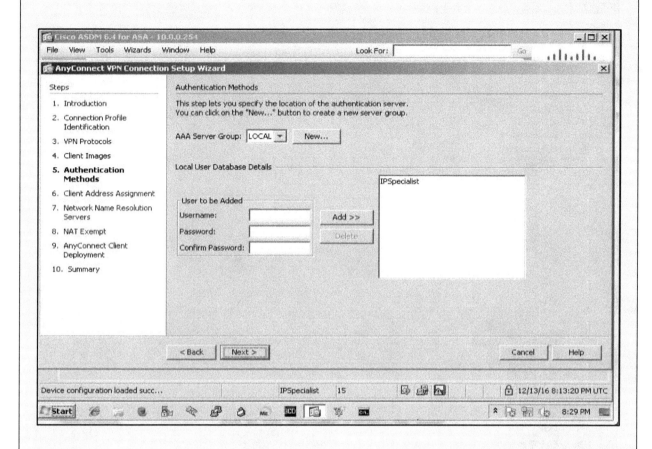

In the diagram above, AAA Server Group LOCAL is selected by default, which means that local database on ASA will be used for authenticating users who want to connect via VPN. Other options include integration with ACS etc. Define the username with   following credentials:

Username: Remote-User

Password: P@$$word:10

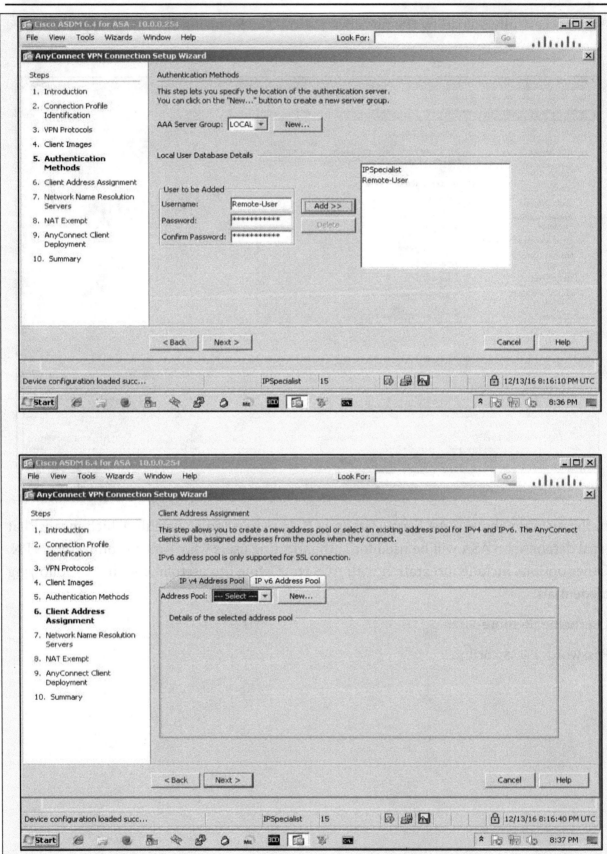

In the above figure, click "New" to define a pool of IP addresses, which will be used to assign IP to connected clients. Use 172.16.0.127 - 172.16.0.254 /24.

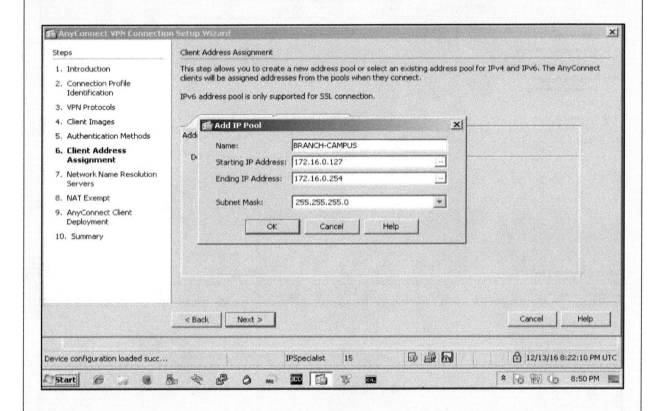

Click "Next" to continue.

Although DNS server is not needed in our lab scenario, use the outside interface IP address and ipspecialist.net as domain name, as shown below:

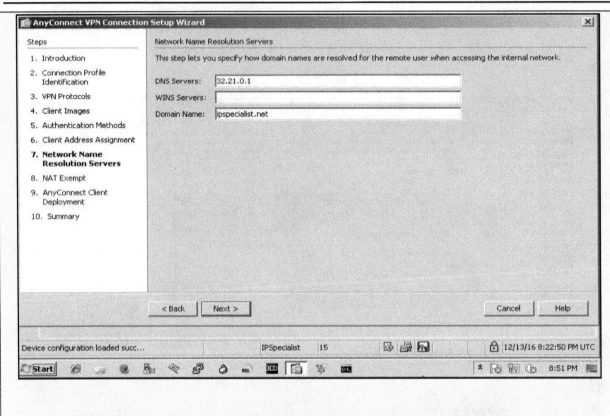

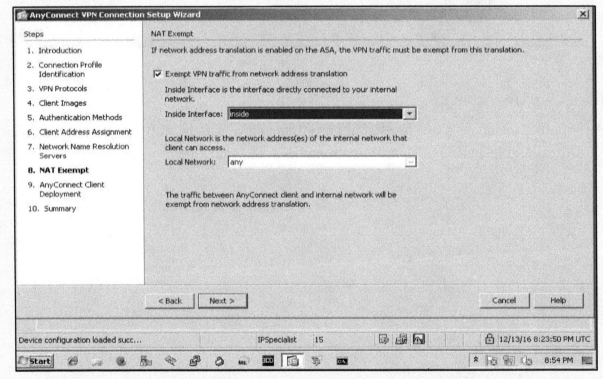

As Real Public Internet Cloud is not involved in our case, it is safe to exempt the traffic coming from Inside interface to be exempted from being NAT. Click "Next".

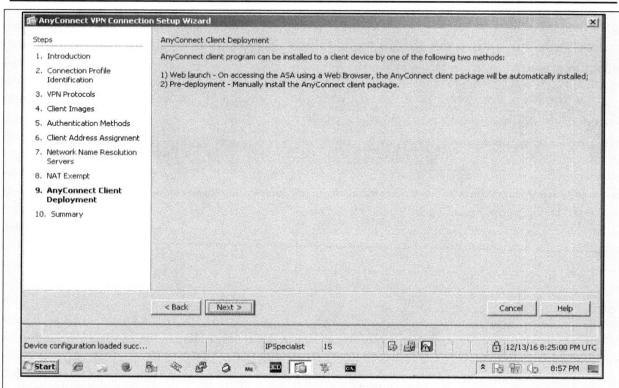

Above figure shows the two methods of AnyConnect client side deployment. Web Launch will be used in this lab.

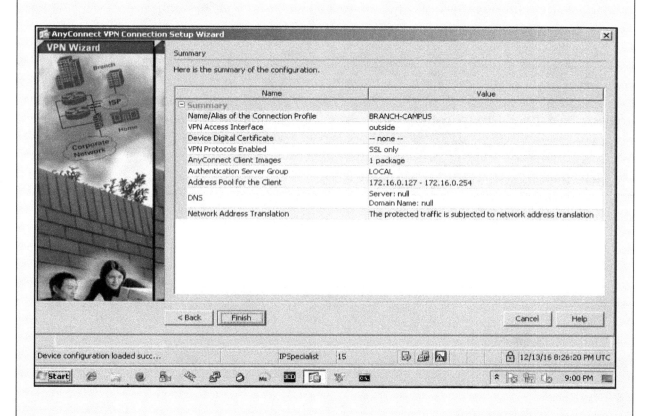

The above figure shows the overall summary of configured SSL AnyConnect VPN. Click "Finish" and jump to Branch Office Management Station for client side configuration.

Open the web browser and enter the outside interface IP address of ASA for secure access. The following web page should appear:

Select the defined Group in above procedure. Use the following credentials to login:

Username: Remote-User

Password: P@$$word:10

Implementing Software Remote Access IPSec VPN (EZVPN)

Case Study

In this lab, we are going to Implement EZVPN using CSR1000v router. CSR1000v router requires 5g security license to support the commands used in this lab.

Topology Diagram:

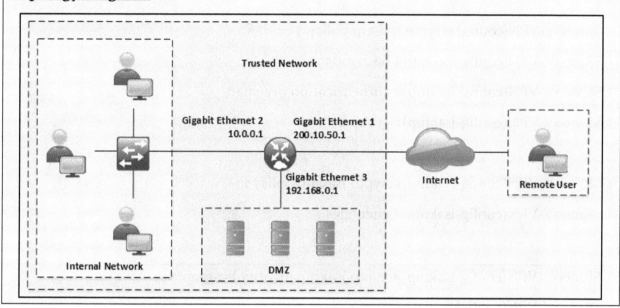

EZVPN Configuration

Router(config)#hostname CSR1000V-VPN

CSR1000V-VPN(config)#enable password password@123

CSR1000V-VPN(config)#aaa new-model

CSR1000V-VPN(config)#aaa authentication login userlist group radius local

CSR1000V-VPN(config)#aaa authorization network grouplist local

CSR1000V-VPN(config)#aaa session-id common

CSR1000V-VPN(config)#ip domain name ipspecialist.net

```
CSR1000V-VPN(config)#username admin privilege 15 password 0 Cisco123

CSR1000V-VPN(config)#username user123 password 0 password123


CSR1000V-VPN(config)#ip scp server enable


CSR1000V-VPN(config)#crypto isakmp policy 3

CSR1000V-VPN(config-isakmp)# hash md5

CSR1000V-VPN(config-isakmp)# authentication pre-share

CSR1000V-VPN(config-isakmp)# group 2


CSR1000V-VPN(config-isakmp)#crypto isakmp policy 10

CSR1000V-VPN(config-isakmp)# encr 3des
```

```
CSR1000V-VPN(config-isakmp)#crypto isakmp identity hostname

CSR1000V-VPN(config)#crypto isakmp client configuration group ipspecialist

CSR1000V-VPN(config-isakmp-group)# key ipspecialist@123

CSR1000V-VPN(config-isakmp-group)# pool pool1

CSR1000V-VPN(config-isakmp-group)# acl 199


CSR1000V-VPN(config-isakmp-group)#Crypto ipsec transform-set set1 esp-3des esp-md5-hmac

CSR1000V-VPN(cfg-crypto-trans)# mode tunnel


CSR1000V-VPN(cfg-crypto-trans)#crypto dynamic-map mode 1

CSR1000V-VPN(config-crypto-map)# set transform-set set1

CSR1000V-VPN(config-crypto-map)# reverse-route


CSR1000V-VPN(config-crypto-map)#crypto map mode client authentication list userlist

CSR1000V-VPN(config)#crypto map mode isakmp authorization list grouplist
```

CSR1000V-VPN(config)#crypto map mode client configuration address respond

CSR1000V-VPN(config)#crypto map mode 1 ipsec-isakmp dynamic mode

CSR1000V-VPN(config)#interface GigabitEthernet1

CSR1000V-VPN(config-if)# ip address 200.10.50.1 255.255.255.0

CSR1000V-VPN(config-if)# ip nat outside

CSR1000V-VPN(config-if)# negotiation auto

CSR1000V-VPN(config-if)# crypto map mode

CSR1000V-VPN(config-if)#interface GigabitEthernet2

CSR1000V-VPN(config-if)# description #Internal Network#

CSR1000V-VPN(config-if)# ip address 10.0.0.1 255.0.0.0

CSR1000V-VPN(config-if)# ip nat inside

CSR1000V-VPN(config-if)# negotiation auto

CSR1000V-VPN(config-if)#interface GigabitEthernet3

CSR1000V-VPN(config-if)# description #DMZ-Internal-Servers#

CSR1000V-VPN(config-if)# ip address 192.168.0.1 255.255.255.0

CSR1000V-VPN(config-if)# ip nat inside

CSR1000V-VPN(config-if)# negotiation auto

CSR1000V-VPN(config-if)#ip local pool pool1 192.168.20.1 192.168.20.100

CSR1000V-VPN(config)#$list LAN-To-INT interface GigabitEthernet1 overload

CSR1000V-VPN(config)#ip forward-protocol nd

CSR1000V-VPN(config)#no ip http server

CSR1000V-VPN(config)#no ip http secure-server

CSR1000V-VPN(config)#ip route 0.0.0.0 0.0.0.0 200.10.50.1

```
CSR1000V-VPN(config)#ip access-list extended LAN-To-INT

CSR1000V-VPN(config-ext-nacl)# deny ip 10.0.0.0 0.255.255.255 192.168.20.0 0.0.0.255

CSR1000V-VPN(config-ext-nacl)# deny ip 10.0.0.0 0.0.0.255 192.168.0.0 0.0.0.255

CSR1000V-VPN(config-ext-nacl)# deny ip 192.168.0.0 0.0.0.255 192.168.20.0 0.0.0.255

CSR1000V-VPN(config-ext-nacl)# permit ip 10.0.0.0 0.0.0.255 any

CSR1000V-VPN(config-ext-nacl)# permit ip 192.168.0.0 0.0.0.255 any


CSR1000V-VPN(config-ext-nacl)#access-list 199 permit ip 10.0.0.0 0.0.0.255 any

CSR1000V-VPN(config)#access-list 199 permit ip 192.168.0.0 0.0.0.255 any


CSR1000V-VPN(config)#radius-server host 192.168.0.10

Warning: The CLI will be deprecated soon

'radius-server host 192.168.10.10'

Please move to 'radius server <name>' CLI.

CSR1000V-VPN(config)#radius-server key admin@ips

CSR1000V-VPN(config)#

*Feb 26 04:03:15.749: %CRYPTO-6-ISAKMP_ON_OFF: ISAKMP is ON
```

AnyConnect VPN Client Configuration & Verification

Open Cisco AnyConnect Client Application on the remote Windows PC.

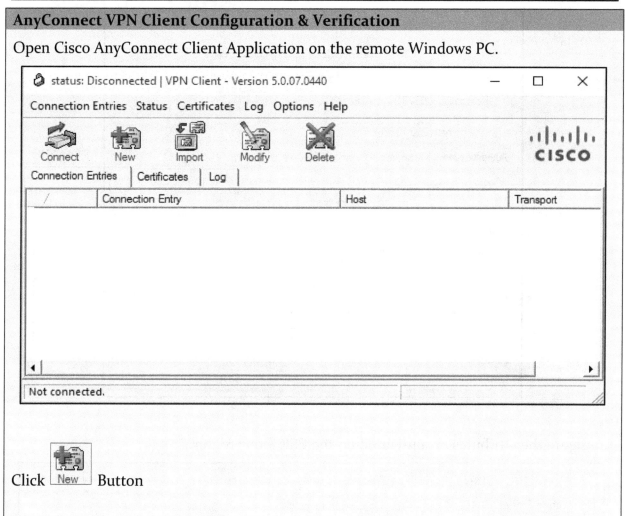

Click Button

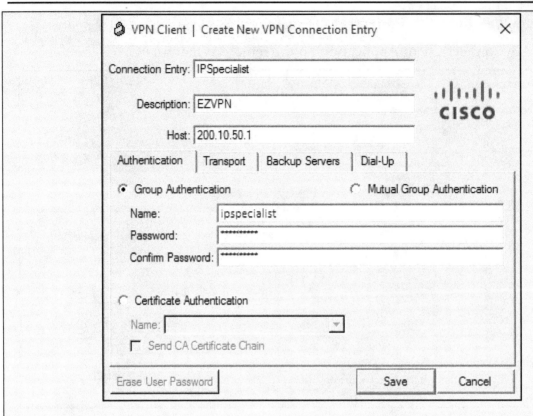

Configure the attributes as configured on the CSR 1000v router.

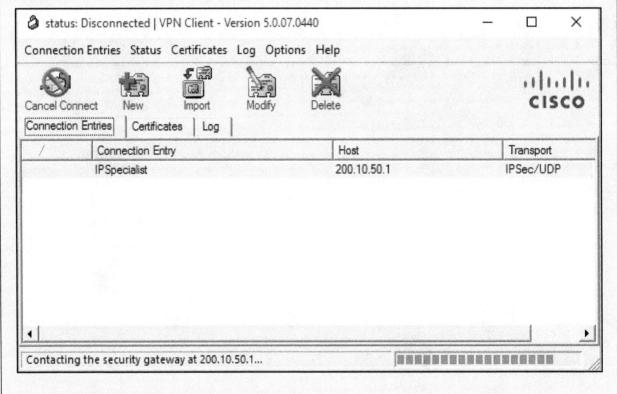

Click [Connect] button to connect to the VPN.

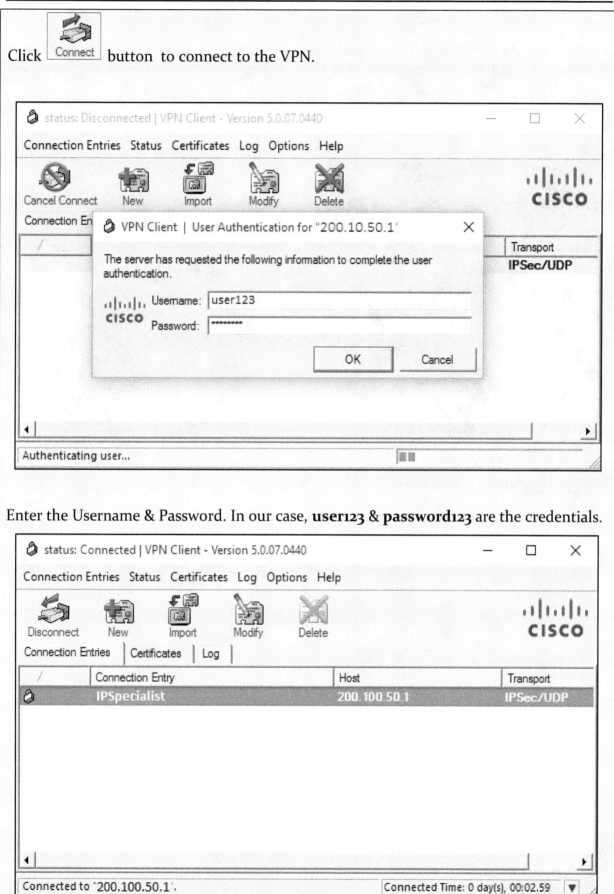

Enter the Username & Password. In our case, **user123** & **password123** are the credentials.

AnyConnect client will now show successful connection to the remote VPN network. You may have to disable the firewall and edit registry settings depending upon the version of windows and its fixes.

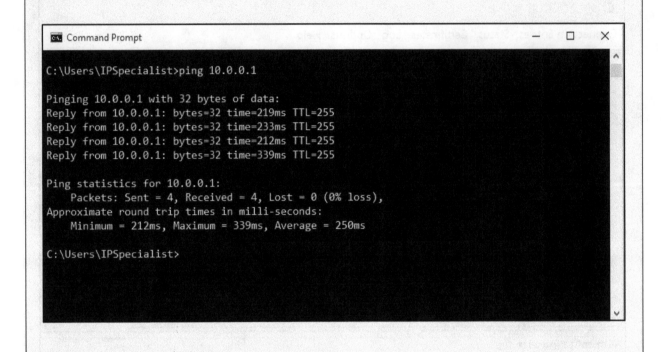

Pinging the remote network is successful!

Chapter 3: Troubleshooting & Monitoring VPN

Troubleshooting VPN

Troubleshooting IPSEC IKEv1 based on Configuration Output

This troubleshooting is performed on Lab 1.1, **Implementing IPv4 IPSec with IKEv1**.

Troubleshooting IPSec (IKEv1)

Show crypto isakmp sa command, which shows Internet Security Association Management Protocol (ISAKMP) Security Associations (SAs) built between peers.

```
ASA                                                        —    □    ✕

ASA#
ASA# show crypto isakmp sa

IKEv1 SAs:

    Active SA: 1
    Rekey SA: 0 (A tunnel will report 1 Active and 1 Rekey SA during rekey)
Total IKE SA: 1

1   IKE Peer: 1.0.0.2
    Type   : L2L          Role    : initiator
    Rekey  : no           State   : MM_ACTIVE

There are no IKEv2 SAs
ASA# ▮
```

The show crypto isakmp sa command shows the current IKE SAs. "Active" status means ISAKMP SA is in active state. The Source IP address indicates which endpoint initiated the IKE negotiation, and IKEv1 SAs showsIKEv1 is in used. If there is any other VPN configuration using IKEv2, it will be mentioned in the above output at the end.

Show vpn-sessiondb Commnad Shows active VPN session information.

```
ASA                                                              —    □    ✕

ASA# show vpn-sessiondb
-------------------------------------------------------------------
VPN Session Summary
-------------------------------------------------------------------
                        Active : Cumulative : Peak Concur : Inactive
                        ---------------------------------------------
Site-to-Site VPN      :    1 :           1 :            1
   IKEv1 IPsec        :    1 :           1 :            1
                        ---------------------------------------------
Total Active and Inactive :    1          Total Cumulative :      1
Device Total VPN Capacity :    0
Device Load           :   0%
***!! WARNING: Platform capacity exceeded !!***
-------------------------------------------------------------------


-------------------------------------------------------------------
Tunnels Summary
-------------------------------------------------------------------
                        Active : Cumulative : Peak Concurrent
                        ---------------------------------------------
IKEv1                 :    1 :           1 :            1
IPsec                 :    1 :           1 :            1
                        ---------------------------------------------
Totals                :    2 :           2
-------------------------------------------------------------------

ASA#
```

Show crypto ipsec sa peer 1.0.0.2

```
ASA                                                        —    □    ✕

ASA# show crypto ipsec sa peer 1.0.0.2
peer address: 1.0.0.2
    Crypto map tag: IPSEC-CRYPTOMAP, seq num: 10, local addr: 172.16.1.1

      access-list VPN-ACL extended permit ip 10.0.0.0 255.0.0.0 11.0.0.0 255.0.0
.0
      local ident (addr/mask/prot/port): (10.0.0.0/255.0.0.0/0/0)
      remote ident (addr/mask/prot/port): (11.0.0.0/255.0.0.0/0/0)
      current_peer: 1.0.0.2

      #pkts encaps: 19, #pkts encrypt: 19, #pkts digest: 19
      #pkts decaps: 18, #pkts decrypt: 18, #pkts verify: 18
      #pkts compressed: 0, #pkts decompressed: 0
      #pkts not compressed: 19, #pkts comp failed: 0, #pkts decomp failed: 0
      #pre-frag successes: 0, #pre-frag failures: 0, #fragments created: 0
      #PMTUs sent: 0, #PMTUs rcvd: 0, #decapsulated frgs needing reassembly: 0
      #send errors: 0, #recv errors: 0

      local crypto endpt.: 172.16.1.1/0, remote crypto endpt.: 1.0.0.2/0
      path mtu 1500, ipsec overhead 58, media mtu 1500
      current outbound spi: 4CB40C1B
      current inbound spi : 03C7CD03

    inbound esp sas:
      spi: 0x03C7CD03 (63425795)
         transform: esp-des esp-md5-hmac no compression
         in use settings ={L2L, Tunnel, }
         slot: 0, conn_id: 4096, crypto-map: IPSEC-CRYPTOMAP
         sa timing: remaining key lifetime (kB/sec): (4373998/3450)
         IV size: 8 bytes
         replay detection support: Y
         Anti replay bitmap:
          0x00000000 0x0007FFFF
    outbound esp sas:
      spi: 0x4CB40C1B (1286867995)
         transform: esp-des esp-md5-hmac no compression
         in use settings ={L2L, Tunnel, }
         slot: 0, conn_id: 4096, crypto-map: IPSEC-CRYPTOMAP
         sa timing: remaining key lifetime (kB/sec): (4373998/3450)
         IV size: 8 bytes
         replay detection support: Y
         Anti replay bitmap:
          0x00000000 0x00000001

ASA#
```

Show vpn-sessiondb detail l2l filter ipaddress 1.0.0.2

```
 ASA                                                      —    □    ×

ASA# show vpn-sessiondb detail l2l filter ipaddress 1.0.0.2

Session Type: LAN-to-LAN Detailed


Connection  : 1.0.0.2
Index       : 1                      IP Addr      : 1.0.0.2
Protocol    : IKEv1 IPsec
Encryption  : DES                    Hashing      : MD5
Bytes Tx    : 1596                   Bytes Rx     : 1512
Login Time  : 10:55:40 UTC Thu Jul 6 2017
Duration    : 0h:02m:54s
IKEv1 Tunnels: 1
IPsec Tunnels: 1

IKEv1:
  Tunnel ID    : 1.1
  UDP Src Port : 500                 UDP Dst Port : 500
  IKE Neg Mode : Main                Auth Mode    : preSharedKeys
  Encryption   : DES                 Hashing      : MD5
  Rekey Int (T): 3600 Seconds        Rekey Left(T): 3426 Seconds
  D/H Group    : 2
  Filter Name  :
  IPv6 Filter  :

IPsec:
  Tunnel ID    : 1.2
  Local Addr   : 10.0.0.0/255.0.0.0/0/0
  Remote Addr  : 11.0.0.0/255.0.0.0/0/0
  Encryption   : DES                 Hashing      : MD5
  Encapsulation: Tunnel
  Rekey Int (T): 3600 Seconds        Rekey Left(T): 3426 Seconds
  Rekey Int (D): 4608000 K-Bytes     Rekey Left(D): 4607999 K-Bytes
  Idle Time Out: 30 Minutes          Idle TO Left : 27 Minutes
  Bytes Tx     : 1596                Bytes Rx     : 1512
  Pkts Tx      : 19                  Pkts Rx      : 18

NAC:
  Reval Int (T): 0 Seconds           Reval Left(T): 0 Seconds
  SQ Int (T)   : 0 Seconds           EoU Age(T)   : 176 Seconds
  Hold Left (T): 0 Seconds           Posture Token:
  Redirect URL :

ASA#
```

Show crypto ipsec sa peer 172.16.1.1

```
37255                                                    —    □    ×

Site#show crypto ipsec sa peer 172.16.1.1

interface: FastEthernet0/0
    Crypto map tag: IPSEC-CRYPTOMAP, local addr 1.0.0.2

  protected vrf: (none)
  local  ident (addr/mask/prot/port): (11.0.0.0/255.0.0.0/0/0)
  remote ident (addr/mask/prot/port): (10.0.0.0/255.0.0.0/0/0)
  current_peer 172.16.1.1 port 500
    PERMIT, flags={origin_is_acl,}
  #pkts encaps: 18, #pkts encrypt: 18, #pkts digest: 18
  #pkts decaps: 19, #pkts decrypt: 19, #pkts verify: 19
  #pkts compressed: 0, #pkts decompressed: 0
  #pkts not compressed: 0, #pkts compr. failed: 0
  #pkts not decompressed: 0, #pkts decompress failed: 0
  #send errors 0, #recv errors 0

   local crypto endpt.: 1.0.0.2, remote crypto endpt.: 172.16.1.1
   path mtu 1500, ip mtu 1500, ip mtu idb FastEthernet0/0
   current outbound spi: 0x3C7CD03(63425795)

   inbound esp sas:
    spi: 0x4CB40C1B(1286867995)
      transform: esp-des esp-md5-hmac ,
      in use settings ={Tunnel, }
      conn id: 1, flow_id: SW:1, crypto map: IPSEC-CRYPTOMAP
      sa timing: remaining key lifetime (k/sec): (4449867/2661)
      IV size: 8 bytes
      replay detection support: Y
      Status: ACTIVE

   inbound ah sas:

   inbound pcp sas:

   outbound esp sas:
    spi: 0x3C7CD03(63425795)
      transform: esp-des esp-md5-hmac ,
      in use settings ={Tunnel, }
      conn id: 2, flow_id: SW:2, crypto map: IPSEC-CRYPTOMAP
      sa timing: remaining key lifetime (k/sec): (4449867/2661)
      IV size: 8 bytes
      replay detection support: Y
      Status: ACTIVE

   outbound ah sas:

   outbound pcp sas:
Site#
```

Show crypto session remote 172.16.1.1 detail

```
🖳 37255                                                    —    ☐    ✕

Site#show crypto session remote 172.16.1.1 detail
Crypto session current status

Code: C - IKE Configuration mode, D - Dead Peer Detection
K - Keepalives, N - NAT-traversal, X - IKE Extended Authentication
F - IKE Fragmentation

Interface: FastEthernet0/0
Uptime: 00:18:03
Session status: UP-ACTIVE
Peer: 172.16.1.1 port 500 fvrf: (none) ivrf: (none)
      Phase1_id: 172.16.1.1
      Desc: (none)
  IKE SA: local 1.0.0.2/500 remote 172.16.1.1/500 Active
        Capabilities:(none) connid:1001 lifetime:00:41:55
  IPSEC FLOW: permit ip 11.0.0.0/255.0.0.0 10.0.0.0/255.0.0.0
        Active SAs: 2, origin: crypto map
        Inbound:  #pkts dec'ed 19 drop 0 life (KB/Sec) 4449867/2516
        Outbound: #pkts enc'ed 18 drop 0 life (KB/Sec) 4449867/2516

Site#█
```

Debug crypto isakmp

```
🖳 37255                                                    —    ☐    ✕

Crypto ISAKMP debugging is on
Site#
*Mar  1 00:37:11.051: ISAKMP:(1001):purging node -518160409
*Mar  1 00:37:15.363: ISAKMP (0:1001): received packet from 172.16.1.1 dport 500
 sport 500 Global (R) QM_IDLE
*Mar  1 00:37:15.363: ISAKMP: set new node -707291693 to QM_IDLE
*Mar  1 00:37:15.367: ISAKMP:(1001): processing HASH payload. message ID = -7072
91693
*Mar  1 00:37:15.367: ISAKMP:(1001): processing NOTIFY DPD/R_U_THERE protocol 1
        spi 0, message ID = -707291693, sa = 666BA708
*Mar  1 00:37:15.371: ISAKMP:(1001):deleting node -707291693 error FALSE reason
"Informational (in) state 1"
*Mar  1 00:37:15.371: ISAKMP:(1001):Input = IKE_MESG_FROM_PEER, IKE_INFO_NOTIFY
*Mar  1 00:37:15.371: ISAKMP:(1001):Old State = IKE_P1_COMPLETE  New State = IKE
_P1_COMPLETE

*Mar  1 00:37:15.375: ISAKMP:(1001):DPD/R_U_THERE received from peer 172.16.1.1,
 sequence 0x202229BE
*Mar  1 00:37:15.379: ISAKMP: set new node -1954133421 to QM_IDLE
*Mar  1 00:37:15.379: ISAKMP:(1001):Sending NOTIFY DPD/R_U_THERE_ACK protocol 1
        spi 1725839192, message ID = -1954133421
*Mar  1 00:37:15.379: ISAKMP:(1001): seq. no 0x202229BE
*Mar  1 00:37:15.383: ISAKMP:(1001): sending packet to 172.16.1.1 my_port 500 pe
er_port 500 (R) QM_IDLE
*Mar  1 00:37:15.383: ISAKMP:(1001):Sending an IKE IPv4 Packet.
*Mar  1 00:37:15.383: ISAKMP:(1001):purging node -1954133421
*Mar  1 00:37:15.387: ISAKMP:(1001):Input = IKE_MESG_FROM_PEER, IKE_MESG_KEEP_AL
IVE
```

Troubleshooting IPSEC IKEv2 based on Configuration Output

This troubleshooting is performed on Lab 1.2, **Implementing IPv4 IPSec with IKEv2.**

Troubleshooting:

Site1# show crypto ikev2 session

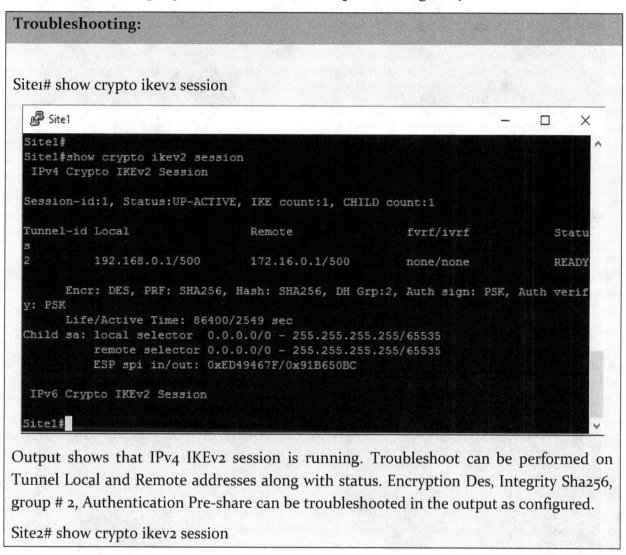

Output shows that IPv4 IKEv2 session is running. Troubleshoot can be performed on Tunnel Local and Remote addresses along with status. Encryption Des, Integrity Sha256, group # 2, Authentication Pre-share can be troubleshooted in the output as configured.

Site2# show crypto ikev2 session

```
                                                                    Site2                    —    □    ×

Site2#show crypto ikev2 session
 IPv4 Crypto IKEv2 Session

Session-id:1, Status:UP-ACTIVE, IKE count:1, CHILD count:1

Tunnel-id Local                  Remote                 fvrf/ivrf              Statu
s
1        172.16.0.1/500          192.168.0.1/500        none/none              READY

      Encr: DES, PRF: SHA256, Hash: SHA256, DH Grp:2, Auth sign: PSK, Auth verif
y: PSK
      Life/Active Time: 86400/2622 sec
Child sa: local selector  0.0.0.0/0 - 255.255.255.255/65535
         remote selector 0.0.0.0/0 - 255.255.255.255/65535
         ESP spi in/out: 0x91B650BC/0xED49467F

 IPv6 Crypto IKEv2 Session

Site2#
```

Site1# show crypto ikev2 session detail

```
                                                                    Site1                    —    □    ×

Site1#show crypto ikev2 session detail
 IPv4 Crypto IKEv2 Session

Session-id:1, Status:UP-ACTIVE, IKE count:1, CHILD count:1

Tunnel-id Local                  Remote                 fvrf/ivrf              Status
2        192.168.0.1/500         172.16.0.1/500         none/none              READY
      Encr: DES, PRF: SHA256, Hash: SHA256, DH Grp:2, Auth sign: PSK, Auth verify: PSK
      Life/Active Time: 86400/2680 sec
      CE id: 1002, Session-id: 1
      Status Description: Negotiation done
      Local spi: 7124331AA950B1F6       Remote spi: 1EA815325BCDC29F
      Local id: ipspecialist1.net
      Remote id: ipspecialist2.net
      Local req msg id:  0             Remote req msg id:  2
      Local next msg id: 0             Remote next msg id: 2
      Local req queued:  0             Remote req queued:  2
      Local window:      5             Remote window:      5
      DPD configured for 0 seconds, retry 0
      Fragmentation not configured.
      Extended Authentication not configured.
      NAT-T is not detected
      Cisco Trust Security SGT is disabled
      Initiator of SA : No
Child sa: local selector  0.0.0.0/0 - 255.255.255.255/65535
         remote selector 0.0.0.0/0 - 255.255.255.255/65535
         ESP spi in/out: 0xED49467F/0x91B650BC
         AH spi in/out: 0x0/0x0
         CPI in/out: 0x0/0x0
         Encr: 3DES, esp_hmac: SHA96
         ah_hmac: None, comp: IPCOMP_NONE, mode tunnel

 IPv6 Crypto IKEv2 Session

Site1#
```

Output with detail command shows all parameters as above, including Lifetime, Active time, CE id, Session ID, Status, Local and Remote fqdn as well as the initiator of this session. As shown, this router is not the initiator.

Site2# show crypto ikev2 session detail

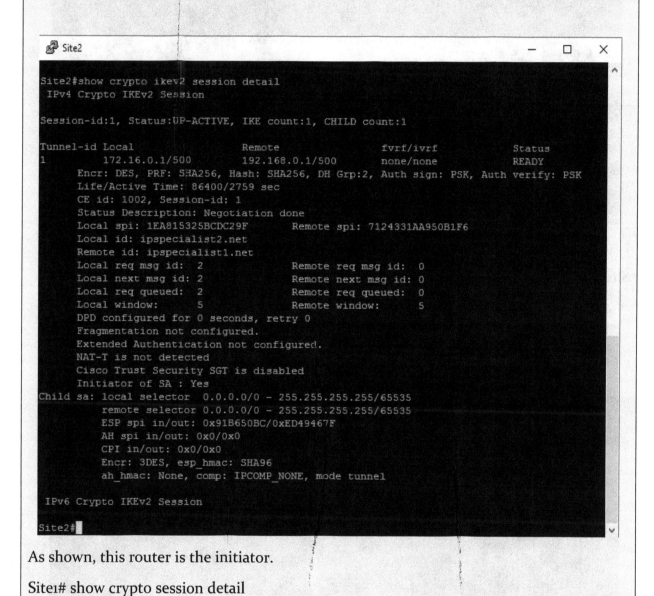

```
Site2#show crypto ikev2 session detail
 IPv4 Crypto IKEv2 Session

Session-id:1, Status:UP-ACTIVE, IKE count:1, CHILD count:1

Tunnel-id Local                     Remote                  fvrf/ivrf            Status
1         172.16.0.1/500            192.168.0.1/500         none/none            READY
      Encr: DES, PRF: SHA256, Hash: SHA256, DH Grp:2, Auth sign: PSK, Auth verify: PSK
      Life/Active Time: 86400/2759 sec
      CE id: 1002, Session-id: 1
      Status Description: Negotiation done
      Local spi: 1EA815325BCDC29F        Remote spi: 7124331AA950B1F6
      Local id: ipspecialist2.net
      Remote id: ipspecialist1.net
      Local req msg id:  2              Remote req msg id:  0
      Local next msg id: 2              Remote next msg id: 0
      Local req queued:  2              Remote req queued:  0
      Local window:      5              Remote window:      5
      DPD configured for 0 seconds, retry 0
      Fragmentation not configured.
      Extended Authentication not configured.
      NAT-T is not detected
      Cisco Trust Security SGT is disabled
      Initiator of SA : Yes
Child sa: local selector  0.0.0.0/0 - 255.255.255.255/65535
          remote selector 0.0.0.0/0 - 255.255.255.255/65535
          ESP spi in/out: 0x91B650BC/0xED49467F
          AH spi in/out: 0x0/0x0
          CPI in/out: 0x0/0x0
          Encr: 3DES, esp_hmac: SHA96
          ah_hmac: None, comp: IPCOMP_NONE, mode tunnel

 IPv6 Crypto IKEv2 Session

Site2#
```

As shown, this router is the initiator.

Site1# show crypto session detail

```
Site1                                                          —    □    ✕

Site1#show crypto session detail
Crypto session current status

Code: C - IKE Configuration mode, D - Dead Peer Detection
K - Keepalives, N - NAT-traversal, T - cTCP encapsulation
X - IKE Extended Authentication, F - IKE Fragmentation
R - IKE Auto Reconnect

Interface: Tunnel0
Profile: IKEv2-Profile
Uptime: 00:47:04
Session status: UP-ACTIVE
Peer: 172.16.0.1 port 500 fvrf: (none) ivrf: (none)
      Phase1_id: ipspecialist2.net
      Desc: (none)
  Session ID: 2
  IKEv2 SA: local 192.168.0.1/500 remote 172.16.0.1/500 Active
            Capabilities:(none) connid:2 lifetime:23:12:56
  IPSEC FLOW: permit ip 0.0.0.0/0.0.0.0 0.0.0.0/0.0.0.0
      Active SAs: 2, origin: crypto map
      Inbound:  #pkts dec'ed 229 drop 0 life (KB/Sec) 4373646/775
      Outbound: #pkts enc'ed 244 drop 0 life (KB/Sec) 4373645/775

Site1#
```

Number of detected and dropped packets can be troubleshooted using this command:

Site2# show crypto session detail

```
Site2                                                          —    □    ✕

Site2#show crypto session detail
Crypto session current status

Code: C - IKE Configuration mode, D - Dead Peer Detection
K - Keepalives, N - NAT-traversal, T - cTCP encapsulation
X - IKE Extended Authentication, F - IKE Fragmentation
R - IKE Auto Reconnect

Interface: Tunnel0
Profile: IKEv2-Profile
Uptime: 00:47:46
Session status: UP-ACTIVE
Peer: 192.168.0.1 port 500 fvrf: (none) ivrf: (none)
      Phase1_id: ipspecialist1.net
      Desc: (none)
  Session ID: 1
  IKEv2 SA: local 172.16.0.1/500 remote 192.168.0.1/500 Active
            Capabilities:(none) connid:1 lifetime:23:12:14
  IPSEC FLOW: permit ip 0.0.0.0/0.0.0.0 0.0.0.0/0.0.0.0
      Active SAs: 2, origin: crypto map
      Inbound:  #pkts dec'ed 241 drop 0 life (KB/Sec) 4357587/733
      Outbound: #pkts enc'ed 243 drop 0 life (KB/Sec) 4357586/733

Site2#
```

Troubleshooting DMVPN based on Configuration Output

This troubleshooting is performed on Lab 1.3, **Implementing DMVPN IPv4 Hub-Spoke and Spoke-Spoke**.

Troubleshooting:

R2# show ip route bgp 65000

As we configure bgp for tunnel 0, 10.0.0.0/8 and 12.0.0.0/8, networks are successfully learned by Spoke Router 2.

R3# show nhrp detail

Next Hop details:

R2# show dmvpn detail

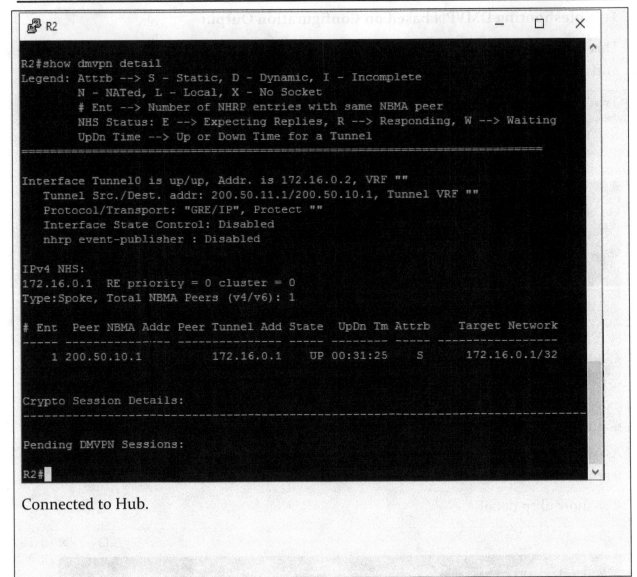

Connected to Hub.

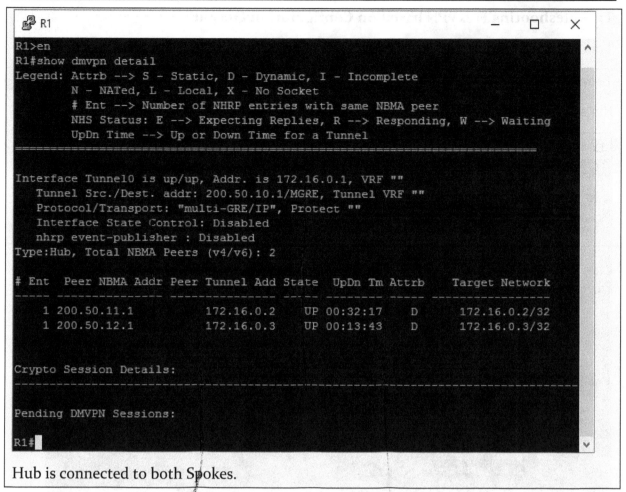

```
R1>en
R1#show dmvpn detail
Legend: Attrb --> S - Static, D - Dynamic, I - Incomplete
        N - NATed, L - Local, X - No Socket
        # Ent --> Number of NHRP entries with same NBMA peer
        NHS Status: E --> Expecting Replies, R --> Responding, W --> Waiting
        UpDn Time --> Up or Down Time for a Tunnel
==========================================================================

Interface Tunnel0 is up/up, Addr. is 172.16.0.1, VRF ""
   Tunnel Src./Dest. addr: 200.50.10.1/MGRE, Tunnel VRF ""
   Protocol/Transport: "multi-GRE/IP", Protect ""
   Interface State Control: Disabled
   nhrp event-publisher : Disabled
Type:Hub, Total NBMA Peers (v4/v6): 2

# Ent  Peer NBMA Addr Peer Tunnel Add State  UpDn Tm Attrb    Target Network
----- --------------- ---------------- ----- --------- -----  ----------------
    1 200.50.11.1        172.16.0.2      UP  00:32:17   D      172.16.0.2/32
    1 200.50.12.1        172.16.0.3      UP  00:13:43   D      172.16.0.3/32


Crypto Session Details:
--------------------------------------------------------------------------


Pending DMVPN Sessions:

R1#
```

Hub is connected to both Spokes.

Troubleshooting FlexVPN based on Configuration Output

This troubleshooting is performed on Lab 1.5, **Implementing Site-to-Site FlexVPN**.

Troubleshooting:

R1# **show crypto ikev2 sa detailed**

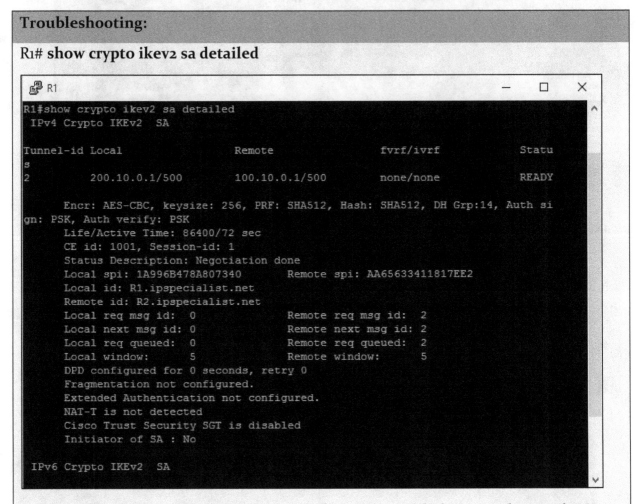

Output shows IPv4 Crypto IKev2 SAs information, including Local tunnel ID i.e. **200.10.0.1** & remote ID i.e. **100.10.0.1**. Status is Ready, Encryption used is **AES-CBC**. Additionally, the output shows Local and Remote SPI information, Local & Remote FQDN information and related parameters. This Router (R1) is not the **initiator of SA**.

R2# **show crypto ikev2 sa detailed**

```
R2                                                              —    □    ×

R2#show crypto ikev2 sa detailed
 IPv4 Crypto IKEv2  SA

Tunnel-id Local                    Remote                  fvrf/ivrf            Statu
s
1        100.10.0.1/500           200.10.0.1/500           none/none            READY
        Encr: AES-CBC, keysize: 256, PRF: SHA512, Hash: SHA512, DH Grp:14, Auth si
gn: PSK, Auth verify: PSK
        Life/Active Time: 86400/195 sec
        CE id: 1001, Session-id: 1
        Status Description: Negotiation done
        Local spi: AA65633411817EE2        Remote spi: 1A996B478A807340
        Local id: R2.ipspecialist.net
        Remote id: R1.ipspecialist.net
        Local req msg id:  2          Remote req msg id:  0
        Local next msg id: 2          Remote next msg id: 0
        Local req queued:  2          Remote req queued:  0
        Local window:      5          Remote window:      5
        DPD configured for 0 seconds, retry 0
        Fragmentation not configured.
        Extended Authentication not configured.
        NAT-T is not detected
        Cisco Trust Security SGT is disabled
        Initiator of SA : Yes

 IPv6 Crypto IKEv2  SA

R2#
```

Similarly, as the commands are executed on another site router, the output shows the same parameters which were discussed before, hence this router (R2) is the *initiator of the SA*.

R2# **show crypto session**

```
R2                                                              —    □    ×

R2#show crypto session
Crypto session current status

Interface: Tunnel0
Profile: IKEPROFILE
Session status: UP-ACTIVE
Peer: 200.10.0.1 port 500
  Session ID: 1
  IKEv2 SA: local 100.10.0.1/500 remote 200.10.0.1/500 Active
  IPSEC FLOW: permit ip 0.0.0.0/0.0.0.0 0.0.0.0/0.0.0.0
       Active SAs: 2, origin: crypto map

R2#
```

Command shows associated interface information *Tunnel 0*, associated profile, *IKEPROFILE*, Session status is *UP and Active*, peer address, port, session ID, and route information.

R1# show crypto session

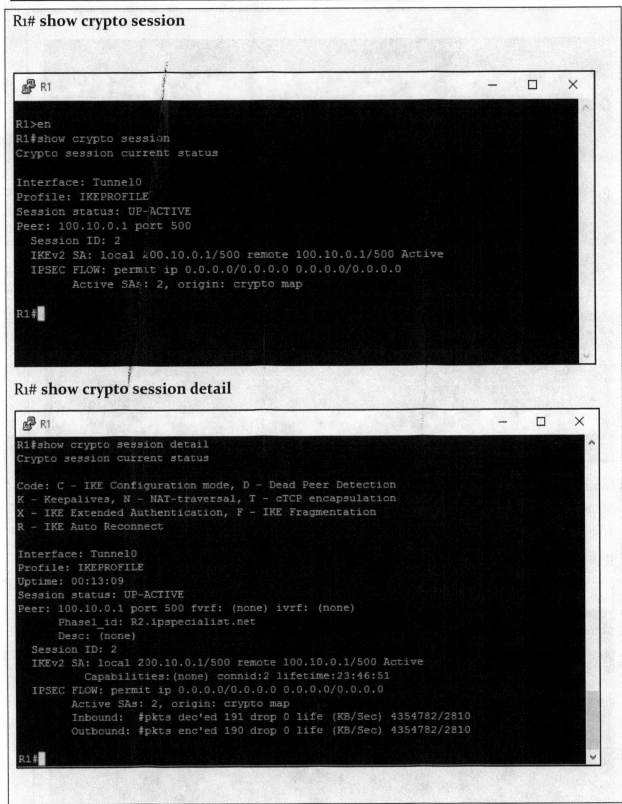

```
R1>en
R1#show crypto session
Crypto session current status

Interface: Tunnel0
Profile: IKEPROFILE
Session status: UP-ACTIVE
Peer: 100.10.0.1 port 500
  Session ID: 2
  IKEv2 SA: local 200.10.0.1/500 remote 100.10.0.1/500 Active
  IPSEC FLOW: permit ip 0.0.0.0/0.0.0.0 0.0.0.0/0.0.0.0
        Active SAs: 2, origin: crypto map

R1#
```

R1# show crypto session detail

```
R1#show crypto session detail
Crypto session current status

Code: C - IKE Configuration mode, D - Dead Peer Detection
K - Keepalives, N - NAT-traversal, T - cTCP encapsulation
X - IKE Extended Authentication, F - IKE Fragmentation
R - IKE Auto Reconnect

Interface: Tunnel0
Profile: IKEPROFILE
Uptime: 00:13:09
Session status: UP-ACTIVE
Peer: 100.10.0.1 port 500 fvrf: (none) ivrf: (none)
     Phase1_id: R2.ipspecialist.net
     Desc: (none)
  Session ID: 2
  IKEv2 SA: local 200.10.0.1/500 remote 100.10.0.1/500 Active
        Capabilities:(none) connid:2 lifetime:23:46:51
  IPSEC FLOW: permit ip 0.0.0.0/0.0.0.0 0.0.0.0/0.0.0.0
        Active SAs: 2, origin: crypto map
        Inbound:  #pkts dec'ed 191 drop 0 life (KB/Sec) 4354782/2810
        Outbound: #pkts enc'ed 190 drop 0 life (KB/Sec) 4354782/2810

R1#
```

References

- http://www.Cisco.com/c/en/us/td/docs/wireless/prime_infrastructure/1-3/configuration/guide/pi_13_cg/ovr.pdf
- http://www.Cisco.com/c/en/us/products/security/security-manager/index.html
- http://www.Cisco.com/c/en/us/about/security-center/dnssec-best-practices.html
- https://tools.ietf.org/html/rfc793
- https://tools.ietf.org/html/rfc1180
- https://www.cisco.com/c/en/us/support/docs/ip/routing-information-protocol-rip/13769-5.html
- https://www.cisco.com/en/US/docs/internetworking/troubleshooting/guide/tr1907.html
- https://www.cisco.com/c/en/us/td/docs/ios-xml/ios/ipapp/configuration/15-mt/iap-15-mt-book/iap-tcp.html
- https://www.cisco.com/c/en/us/td/docs/voice_ip_comm/cucm/port/9_1_1/CUCM_BK_T2CA6EDE_00_tcp-port-usage-guide-91/CUCM_BK_T2CA6EDE_00_tcp-port-usage-guide-91_chapter_01.html
- https://www.cisco.com/c/en/us/td/docs/voice_ip_comm/cucmbe3k/8_6_2/system/cucmbe3k_862/04_port_list.html
- https://www.cisco.com/c/en/us/td/docs/voice_ip_comm/cucm/port/10_0_1/CUCM_BK_T537717B_00_tcp-port-usage-guide-100.html
- https://www.cisco.com/c/en/us/support/docs/ip/domain-name-system-dns/12683-dns-descript.html
- https://www.cisco.com/c/en/us/td/docs/ios-xml/ios/ipaddr_dns/configuration/15-mt/dns-15-mt-book/dns-config-dns.html
- https://www.cisco.com/c/en/us/td/docs/ios-xml/ios/ipaddr_dns/configuration/15-mt/dns-15-mt-book/dns-spl-dns.html
- https://www.cisco.com/c/en/us/td/docs/ios-xml/ios/ipaddr_arp/configuration/15-mt/arp-15-mt-book/arp-config-arp.html
- https://www.cisco.com/c/en/us/td/docs/ios-xml/ios/ipaddr_arp/configuration/15-mt/arp-15-mt-book.pdf
- https://learningnetwork.cisco.com/docs/DOC-23702
- https://www.cisco.com/c/en/us/td/docs/ios-xml/ios/ipaddr_arp/configuration/15-mt/arp-15-mt-book/arp-monitor-arp.html
- https://www.cisco.com/c/en/us/support/docs/ip/dynamic-address-allocation-resolution/13718-5.html
- https://www.cisco.com/c/en/us/td/docs/ios-xml/ios/ipaddr_arp/configuration/12-4/arp-12-4-book/arp-config-arp.html

- https://www.cisco.com/c/dam/en_us/about/ciscoitatwork/borderless_networks/docs/Cloud_Web_Security_IT_Methods.pdf
- https://www.cisco.com/c/en/us/products/security/cloud-web-security/eos-eol-notice-listing.html
- https://www.cisco.com/c/en/us/support/docs/security/cloud-web-security/200437-Cloud-Web-Security-Regional-Redirection.html
- https://tools.cisco.com/security/center/content/CiscoSecurityAdvisory/cisco-sa-20180711-wsa-xss
- https://www.cisco.com/c/en/us/td/docs/security/wsa/wsa11-0/user_guide/b_WSA_UserGuide/b_WSA_UserGuide_chapter_01100.html
- https://tools.cisco.com/security/center/content/CiscoSecurityAdvisory/cisco-sa-20180801-wsa-xss
- https://www.cisco.com/c/en/us/products/security/web-security-appliance/index.html
- https://www.cisco.com/c/en/us/support/security/web-security-appliance/tsd-products-support-series-home.html
- https://www.safaribooksonline.com/library/view/mike-meyers-comptia/9781260026559/
- https://www.safaribooksonline.com/library/view/comptia-security-all-in-one/9781260019292/
- https://www.safaribooksonline.com/library/view/comptia-security-review/9781118922903/
- https://msdn.microsoft.com/en-us/library/ff648641.aspx
- https://www.cisco.com/c/en/us/td/docs/ios/12_2/security/configuration/guide/fsecur_c/scfdenl.html
- https://www.ietf.org/rfc/rfc3704.txt
- http://www.cisco.com/c/en/us/td/docs/solutions/Enterprise/Campus/campover.html#wp737141
- http://www.cisco.com/web/services/downloads/smart-solutions-maximize-federal-capabilities-for-mission-success.pdf
- http://www.cisco.com/c/en/us/support/docs/availability/high-availability/15114-NMS-bestpractice.html
- http://www.ciscopress.com/articles/article.asp?p=2180210&seqNum=5
- http://www.cisco.com/c/en/us/td/docs/wireless/prime_infrastructure/1-3/configuration/guide/pi_13_cg/ovr.pdf
- http://www.cisco.com/c/en/us/products/security/security-manager/index.html
- http://www.cisco.com/c/en/us/about/security-center/dnssec-best-practices.html
- http://www.cisco.com/c/en/us/td/docs/ios-xml/ios/sec_usr_ssh/configuration/15-s/sec-usr-ssh-15-s-book/sec-secure-copy.html
- http://www.ciscopress.com/articles/article.asp?p=25477&seqNum=3
- http://www.cisco.com/c/en/us/products/security/ids-4215-sensor/index.html
- https://docs.microsoft.com/en-us/windows/desktop/memory/comparing-memory-allocation-methods
- https://docs.microsoft.com/en-us/windows/desktop/memory/virtual-address-space
- https://docs.microsoft.com/en-us/windows/desktop/memory/memory-pools

- https://docs.microsoft.com/en-us/windows/desktop/memory/memory-performance-information
- https://docs.microsoft.com/en-us/windows/desktop/memory/virtual-memory-functions
- https://docs.microsoft.com/en-us/windows/desktop/memory/allocating-virtual-memory
- https://docs.microsoft.com/en-us/windows/desktop/memory/heap-functions
- https://docs.microsoft.com/en-us/windows/desktop/memory/about-memory-management
- https://docs.microsoft.com/en-us/sysinternals/downloads/procmon
- https://docs.microsoft.com/en-us/sysinternals/downloads/pslist
- https://docs.microsoft.com/en-us/sysinternals/downloads/pskill
- https://docs.microsoft.com/en-us/sysinternals/downloads/process-explorer
- https://docs.microsoft.com/en-us/sysinternals/downloads/procmon
- https://docs.microsoft.com/en-us/sysinternals/downloads/procdump
- https://docs.microsoft.com/en-us/windows/desktop/memory/comparing-memory-allocation-methods
- https://www.safaribooksonline.com/library/view/mike-meyers-comptia/9781260026559/
- http://www.cisco.com/c/en/us/products/security/security-manager/index.html
- http://www.cisco.com/c/en/us/about/security-center/dnssec-best-practices.html
- http://www.cisco.com/c/en/us/td/docs/ios-xml/ios/sec_usr_ssh/configuration/15-s/sec-usr-ssh-15-s-book/sec-secure-copy.html
- http://www.ciscopress.com/articles/article.asp?p=25477&seqNum=3
- http://www.cisco.com/c/en/us/products/security/ids-4215-sensor/index.html

About Our Products

Other Network & Security related products from IPSpecialist LTD are:

- CCNA Routing & Switching Technology Workbook
- CCNA Security v2 Technology Workbook
- CCNA Service Provider Technology Workbook
- CCDA Technology Workbook
- CCDP Technology Workbook
- CCNP Route Technology Workbook
- CCNP Switch Technology Workbook
- CCNP Troubleshoot Technology Workbook
- CCNP Security SENSS Technology Workbook
- CCNP Security SITCS Technology Workbook
- CCNP Security SISAS Technology Workbook
- CompTIA Network+ Technology Workbook
- CompTIA Security+ v2 Technology Workbook
- Certified Information System Security Professional (CISSP) Technology Workbook
- CCNA CyberOps SECFND Technology Workbook
- Certified Block Chain Expert Technology Workbook
- Certified Cloud Security Professional (CCSP) Technology Workbook
- CompTIA Pentest+ Technology Workbook

Upcoming products are:

- CompTIA A+ Core 1 (220-1001) Technology Workbook
- CompTIA A+ Core 2 (220-1002) Technology Workbook
- CompTIA Cyber Security Analyst CySA+ Technology Workbook
- CompTIA Cloud+ Technology Workbook
- CompTIA Server+ Technology Workbook

www.ingramcontent.com/pod-product-compliance
Lightning Source LLC
Chambersburg PA
CBHW060143060326
40690CB00018B/3963